Clinical Intelligence

as a Shared Language Between Law and Medicine

Michelle Carroll

ISBN: 979-8-952094-13-0

First Edition

Lexcura Summit

www.lexcurasummit.com

Table of Contents

Introduction

Why Law and Medicine Need a Shared Language

I've never met a patient who experienced their own healthcare as a medical record. What they experienced was a journey, and that journey began long before any lawyer got involved.

They remember who they were before they got sick. The first symptom, the uncertainty that followed, the phone calls, the people they spoke with, the reasoning behind finally deciding to seek help. They remember whether anyone actually listened to them, whether they felt reassured, whether their concerns were taken seriously, whether the treatment seemed to be working. Some remember sitting in an emergency department for hours while their condition quietly changed underneath them. Some remember being told a test was normal, going home believing they were safe, and then getting worse. Others remember almost nothing at all — they were too sick, too sedated, too confused — and it's their family who ends up carrying the story, noticing changes that were obvious to them but nearly impossible to find later in the chart.

By the time that story reaches an attorney's desk, it usually isn't a story anymore. It's arrived in pieces.

What you get is rarely one clear, continuous account of what happened to this person. More often it's thousands of pages, written by different professionals, in different departments, sometimes across several healthcare organizations that never spoke to one another. The physician's notes tell one part. Nursing assessments tell another. The medication administration record tells you what was given, but rarely why, and almost never whether it worked. Lab systems will tell you exactly when a result became available, down to the minute, but not always who actually saw it. Imaging reports summarize what a radiologist thought they saw, while the original images sit somewhere else entirely, unread by everyone else on the case.

And that's just the record that makes it into evidence. Phone conversations get reduced to a line or two, if they're documented at all. Portal messages between patient and provider often don't show up in the first production. Transfer logs, audit trails, staffing sheets, device data, internal communications — all of this may exist, all of it may matter, and none of it necessarily arrives with the rest.

Then you're expected to figure out what happened.

As the attorney, you need to know whether someone was responsible for this person's care, whether their response was reasonable, whether something they did or didn't do caused harm, and whether any of it can actually be proven under the rules you have to work within — expert requirements, jurisdiction, deadlines, admissibility, damages, cost, the client sitting across from you wanting answers.

Here's the part that took me a while to really absorb: the sheer size of the record isn't really the problem. The problem is that the record was never built to answer the questions you're now asking of it.

Clinicians document for reasons that have almost nothing to do with litigation. They're recording observations, orders, assessments, treatment, communication, billing, compliance, discharge planning — whatever the next professional down the line needs to know, whatever the organization requires, whatever their fifteen minutes between patients allows them to type. Some entries are thorough. Some are three words long. Some explain the reasoning behind a decision. Most just record the conclusion and leave the reasoning to be inferred, or lost.

The medical record is evidence of the patient's journey. It was never the journey itself.

That gap, between what happened to the patient and what got written down about it, is where this book lives.

I started calling the discipline that grew out of closing that gap Clinical Intelligence, mostly because I needed some name for the structured way I'd found of pulling the patient's experience, the clinical evidence, and the legal questions back into one connected understanding — a way of examining what the records actually establish, what they don't, what's still genuinely uncertain, and what has to be answered before anyone makes a real decision about the case.

I want to be careful about what I'm not claiming. This isn't a way of teaching attorneys to practice medicine, and it doesn't ask clinicians to start making legal judgments, or pretend to replace the opinion of a properly qualified expert. Each profession keeps its own authority. The attorney is still responsible for the law: strategy, procedure, the advice given to the client. The clinician is still responsible for explaining what the evidence means clinically, within the honest limits of their training. The retained expert still owns whatever formal specialty opinion the case requires.

What Clinical Intelligence does is connect those roles rather than replace any of them, and I think that connection matters because, left alone, attorneys and clinicians simply don't approach the same case the same way. Not because either one is careless. They're just trained to ask different questions of the same pages.

A clinician sits down and tries to understand what was actually happening to the patient: the symptoms, the risk that was present, what information was available at the time, how the patient responded to what was tried, whether the picture was evolving, whether the plan still made sense as new information came in. An attorney sits down with the same chart and asks something else — what do these clinical events mean under the law? Duty, breach, causation, damages, whether it can be proven, whether it's worth pursuing. Even when something looks clinically troubling, the attorney still has to work out whether it can be established, whether it's legally significant, and whether it probably changed the outcome.

Both of those questions are necessary. Neither one, by itself, gets you to an answer.

A clinical concern doesn't become legal liability just because a clinician thinks something should have been handled differently. A missed policy doesn't prove that missing it caused the injury. A bad outcome doesn't prove the care was unreasonable, and an admitted mistake doesn't automatically mean that mistake changed anything for the patient. The reverse is just as true. A well-recognized complication isn't automatically unavoidable. Pre-existing disease doesn't mean no additional harm occurred. A normal early test doesn't rule out something that was still developing, and a patient who briefly improved wasn't necessarily out of danger.

These aren't academic distinctions. They shape which records get pulled, which experts get retained, what those experts get asked, and what theory of the case can honestly be advanced. They shape the advice given to the client, too.

If I had to name the single greatest risk in a medical case, it's this: the meaning of the evidence quietly shifts as it moves from one profession to the next. A clinician says earlier treatment might have helped, meaning it remained medically possible, and by the time that observation has been repeated a few times, it's become "probably would have prevented the injury" — a very different claim, and not necessarily one the clinician intended to make. A chart says the patient was "stable," and to someone outside medicine that word sounds reassuring, like things were going well. Clinically it can mean something much narrower: that the patient wasn't actively crashing at that exact moment, propped up by oxygen, medication, fluids, whatever was holding them there. An attorney spots a policy that wasn't followed and reads it as evidence of breach. The clinician may agree the process failed, but still needs to work out whether that failure actually changed the care the patient got, or the outcome they had. The policy is real evidence. It just can't answer the whole question by itself.

Lose the shared language, and these small gaps compound. A narrow clinical concern turns into a sweeping legal allegation over the course of a few retellings. An uncertain causal link gets stated with more confidence every time someone repeats it. A perfectly reasonable disagreement about the medicine gets mistaken for a disagreement about the law, or a legal evidentiary problem gets waved off as a weakness in the underlying clinical theory, when it isn't one at all.

Preventing that slippage is really the whole point of Clinical Intelligence. Attorneys, clinicians, experts, and everyone else touching the case work from the same reconstructed patient journey, while still bringing their own expertise to bear on it. The clinical meaning of the evidence gets explained without turning the clinician into the lawyer. The legal significance gets examined without expecting the lawyer to become the medical expert.

None of this means everyone has to end up agreeing. Attorneys and clinicians still disagree. Two qualified experts can look at the same evidence and land in different places. Records stay incomplete, witnesses remember things differently, and sometimes the medicine genuinely supports more than one honest reading. Sometimes the evidence simply won't support a responsible conclusion either way, and that has to be an acceptable outcome too.

What a shared language does is show you where the disagreement actually lives. Are two people disagreeing about what happened, or about how to interpret the same finding? Are they starting from different assumptions about what the patient's baseline even was? Do they disagree about when the condition became something a reasonable clinician should have caught? Is this really about who was responsible, whether a window for treatment was still open, whether a different response would have changed anything — or is it a dispute about what the clinical evidence means once the law gets applied to it? Until those questions are pulled apart, it's easy for two people to think they're arguing about the same thing when they aren't even close.

That's why the patient has to stay at the center of all this. A single patient might move through primary care, urgent care, an emergency department, imaging, a specialist, a hospital admission, rehabilitation, and then home, and every stop along that road generates its own separate record, seen by professionals who each only glimpsed one piece of a picture that was still forming.

The patient, meanwhile, lived through one continuous experience.

Reconstructing that continuous experience — who this person was before, what changed, what information showed up and when, how people and systems responded to it, whether the response worked, when the risk actually shifted, what else could have been done, and what difference that probably would have made — is, in the end, the whole job.

Sometimes that reconstruction confirms exactly what the case already assumed, and sharpens it, pinpointing the precise moment care crossed the line into unreasonable. Sometimes it reveals that the strongest issue in the case isn't the one the client described when they first walked in, or the one written into the original complaint. A case framed as a failure to diagnose may turn out, on closer look, to really be a failure to reassess. A surgical complication that looked like negligence may have been unavoidable, while a later failure to notice the patient deteriorating is what actually made the injury worse. What looked like one person's mistake may turn out to be a communication breakdown or a systems failure that no individual could reasonably have stopped alone.

And sometimes the honest answer is that the care was reasonable, the condition wasn't yet recognizable, the window for a different response had already closed, or the conduct in question probably didn't change what happened to the patient.

A methodology only earns trust if it's willing to land in any of those places, including the ones that don't help the person who asked for the review. This isn't a way to manufacture allegations or hand someone the conclusion they were hoping for when they picked up the phone. The same questions get asked whether the review is for a plaintiff, a defendant, an insurer, a hospital, or counsel who genuinely doesn't yet know whether the case should go forward at all.

Far from making the work less useful, that discipline is what makes it worth trusting. A conclusion reached only after grappling with the normal findings, the uncertainty, the pre-existing disease, the competing causes, the limits of what treatment can do, and the other reasonable explanations, that conclusion holds up. A strong case doesn't get weaker because someone took the hard evidence seriously. It gets more reliable, because it wasn't built by looking away from it.

The chapters that follow stay close to the patient's journey, because that's genuinely where the legal and clinical questions meet. Along the way, we'll look at how medical evidence actually gets created, why its real meaning so easily gets lost inside the record, how hindsight quietly distorts the way we look back at a case, and why the moment that truly mattered can turn out to be a different moment than the one named in the original allegation.

I also want to be honest about what this can't do. Clinical Intelligence doesn't establish legal duty, negligence, causation, damages, or admissibility on its own. It doesn't replace a specialty opinion, judge a witness's credibility, or turn genuine uncertainty into a certainty the evidence was never going to support. Technology can help organize and analyze all of this, and I use quite a bit of it, but it can't assume professional authority, and it can't replace a person's judgment.

What I'm really after is more modest than it might sound, and I think more valuable for being modest: helping everyone in the room understand what the evidence actually shows, before anyone decides what to do with it.

Law and medicine were never going to become one profession, and they shouldn't. What they need is a reliable way of understanding the same patient. That's what this book is trying to offer.

PART ONE

The Problem

Chapters One Through Five

Chapter One: One Patient, Two Professional Perspectives

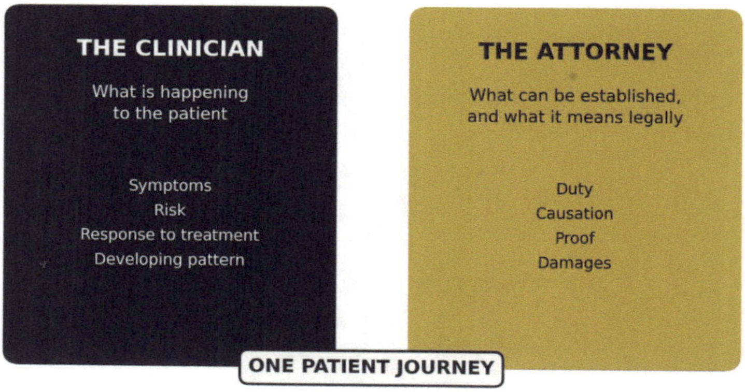

Figure 1.1 — Two lenses, one patient

When an attorney and a clinician sit down with the same medical records, they are not necessarily looking at the same case.

They can be reading the same pages, reviewing the same lab results, following the same sequence of events, and still walk away with completely different ideas about what actually matters. That doesn't mean one of them misread the chart. It usually just means they were trained to look for different things.

The clinician is trying to work out what was happening to the patient. The attorney is trying to work out what can be established about what happened, and what legal weight that carries. Those two questions are related, but they are not the same question, and a lot of the friction in medical cases comes from treating them as though they were.

A clinician tends to go straight to the patient's symptoms, the functional changes, the clinical risk, how the patient responded to treatment, the point where things started to feel more concerning. They're often looking for a pattern that no single note captures on its own but that becomes obvious once you line several findings up next to each other. An attorney, reading that same stack of pages, is looking for responsibility, documentation, contradiction, causation, damages — whether there's actually enough here to support a claim or a defense. Counsel also has to think about expert requirements, procedural rules, what this is going to cost to litigate, what the client expects, and whether the theory can be proved rather than just suspected.

Both of those readings are necessary. The trouble starts when either one gets treated as though it's the whole case by itself. A clinician might flag care that looks troubling without stopping to ask whether that concern can ever be turned into admissible evidence, or whether the thing that went wrong actually caused compensable harm. An attorney might spot an obvious documentation gap or a missed policy and never quite get to the question of whether following the policy would have changed anything for the patient.

The patient sits in between those two ways of thinking about the case. Which is exactly why the patient's own journey has to become the shared point of reference. The patient didn't live through a medical story and a separate legal story. They lived through one continuous course of events — got sick, sought help, received care, ended up somewhere. The medical questions and the legal questions grew up around that same continuous course, even though the two professions come at it from different directions. Clinical Intelligence starts by pulling both of those directions back to that same center.

Clinical professionals spend their careers making decisions before they know how things will turn out. A patient walks in with symptoms that could mean several different things — some serious, some common and self-limiting. The early labs come back normal. The exam is inconclusive. The patient seems to feel a bit better after the first round of treatment. Every clinical decision in that moment gets made inside that uncertainty, without the benefit of knowing what tomorrow holds. The clinician isn't reading the case backward from the outcome. They're asking whether the information in front of them right now is enough to manage this patient safely.

That's a large part of why a clinician tends to read a chart as an unfolding story rather than a series of disconnected decisions. Was the patient improving? Did the symptoms stick around? Did anything new show up? Did the treatment do what it was supposed to do? Did the risk go up instead of down? And, maybe most importantly: was there a point where the original explanation simply stopped fitting the facts?

That last question tends to matter more than whatever the first working diagnosis happened to be. A huge number of cases get described at the outset as a failure to diagnose, when the real issue turns out to live somewhere else entirely. The initial assessment may have been perfectly reasonable — the symptoms genuinely were nonspecific at that point. The real problem surfaces later, when the patient doesn't improve, comes back worse, develops something new, or simply stops fitting the story that justified the original plan. What looks like a failure to diagnose is often, on closer inspection, a failure to reassess. Or a failure to respond to deterioration. Or a failure to pass along a result. Or a failure to notice that the treatment wasn't working and revise a plan that had quietly become unsafe.

These aren't just fine clinical distinctions for their own sake. They determine who needs to be examined, which records actually need to be pulled, which kind of expert the case requires, and whether a different response would probably have changed the outcome. A sweeping allegation can sound compelling in a demand letter. A precise clinical question is almost always more useful in building the case.

The attorney is carrying a different kind of weight. Counsel can't stop at "this looks concerning" — the job is to work out whether the facts add up to something legally viable, which means grappling with duty, departure, causation, damages, whether the evidence actually holds up, and the practical realities of running a piece of litigation. Should this case be taken on at all? Are more records needed? Does it require a specialist, and if so which one? Does the working theory of the case actually match what the medicine shows? Is the likely value of the claim worth the cost and difficulty of pursuing it? Can the opinions this case needs actually be supported in this jurisdiction?

That pressure to get the legal structure in place can push people toward sorting the medical case too quickly. A delay shows up on the timeline, and causation starts to feel assumed. A policy wasn't followed, and breach starts to feel established. The patient got worse after a treatment, and the treatment starts to look like the cause. The patient had a lot of pre-existing disease, and the whole case starts to feel too hard to bother with. Any one of those instincts might turn out to be right in the end. None of them should be assumed before the patient's actual course has been put back together.

The attorney needs enough clinical fluency to know which questions have to be asked — not enough to replace the clinician or the retained expert. Clinical Intelligence was never meant to have counsel interpreting complicated medical evidence on their own. What it offers instead is a structured way of understanding what the evidence actually means, where the real uncertainty sits, and which conclusions genuinely need a professional opinion behind them before anyone relies on them. That makes the legal analysis sharper, not more medical.

Here's something that's easy to lose sight of once a case is broken into exhibits and productions: the patient never experienced their own care as a set of separate records. They called their primary care office, then went to urgent care, had imaging done somewhere else, went home, got worse overnight, ended up in an emergency department, and were eventually transferred to another hospital. To the patient, all of that was one uninterrupted stretch of time. The evidence of that stretch, though, gets scattered across however many separate systems touched the case. Primary care shows the first complaint. Urgent care shows the initial exam. The imaging system holds the original study. The lab platform shows exactly when a result became available. A communication log — if one even exists — might show whether that result was ever routed to someone or acknowledged. The hospital record shows the eventual crisis.

Rehab records often carry the clearest evidence of what the patient actually lost, function-wise, at the end of all of it.

No single one of those records tells the whole story on its own. And when each set gets reviewed in isolation, the case can look entirely different depending on which piece you happen to read first. An emergency department note describing improvement and a discharge home reads one way. A later hospital record that opens with the final diagnosis can make the whole thing look obvious in hindsight, as if anyone should have caught it from the start. Rehab records can show devastating disability without ever explaining how much of that was new versus how much predated the event. A primary care note from months earlier can suddenly look enormously significant — but usually only because you already know the diagnosis that came later, not because it looked that way at the time.

What Clinical Intelligence does is put those fragments back together around the patient, rather than around whichever document happens to be sitting on top of the pile. That changes the whole nature of the review. Instead of asking what each record says in isolation, you're asking how the records fit together — what was actually known at each stage, what was still genuinely uncertain, what changed, and whether the people involved had enough information available to have responded differently. That's how the patient ends up back at the center of the case, instead of the paperwork.

Medical records hold an enormous amount of information, and information only becomes useful once you understand what it means. A blood pressure of 92 over 58 might be completely unremarkable in one patient and deeply concerning in another — and it becomes something else again once you notice it sitting alongside a climbing heart rate, falling urine output, a change in mental status, and a patient who isn't responding to treatment the way they should. A radiology report that says no acute abnormality was identified can sound reassuring on its face. What it actually means depends on which study was done, what condition anyone was even looking for, when it was done relative to the onset of symptoms, whether the original images were ever actually reviewed by someone qualified to catch something subtle, and whether the disease in question could plausibly have been too early to show up yet. A chart note describing a patient as "stable" can read, to someone outside medicine, like the patient was doing fine. Clinically, that patient may have remained seriously ill and simply unchanged for the moment — propped up, possibly, by escalating oxygen, medication, or fluids that were the only reason "stable" was even an option.

The attorney needs the clinician to explain that clinical meaning honestly. The clinician needs the attorney to explain why that meaning actually matters to the legal question being asked. Neither one should be expected to step into the other's role — but each has to understand enough of the other's reasoning to talk about the same case accurately. That, in practical terms, is the whole point of a shared language.

A surprising number of the misunderstandings between law and medicine start with perfectly ordinary words. The words themselves aren't complicated. It's the meaning riding along underneath them that causes the trouble. Possible isn't the same as probable. Stable doesn't necessarily mean improving. A recognized complication isn't automatically an unavoidable one. High risk doesn't mean the outcome was inevitable. Pre-existing disease doesn't mean no new harm occurred on top of it. A delay doesn't mean the beneficial window stayed open the entire time. And a contributing factor isn't the same thing as the sole cause. None of these distinctions sound like much when you're discussing them in the abstract. Inside an actual case, they can be the difference between a theory that holds up and one that doesn't.

Take a phrase like "earlier treatment could have helped." A clinician might mean nothing more than that the treatment was biologically plausible and some benefit remained possible. An attorney, hearing the same sentence, might understand it as "the treatment probably would have prevented the injury." Those are two very different opinions wearing the same words. Getting from one to the other honestly means the conversation has to keep going: what treatment, exactly? When should it have happened? Was this particular patient even eligible to receive it? What benefit could reasonably have been expected — full prevention, or just a less severe outcome? Were there competing causes in play that would have affected the result regardless of what anyone did? Once those questions get answered, the opinion sharpens considerably, and it becomes something you can actually use. Sometimes the evidence supports complete prevention. Sometimes it only supports a reduction in severity, or aggravation of something already happening, or acceleration of an inevitable decline, or a lost opportunity that never guaranteed a different result, or, honestly, no material difference at all. The goal was never to squeeze out the strongest possible conclusion. It's to find the conclusion the evidence can actually carry.

An experienced clinician can often sense, fairly quickly, that something went wrong in a chart. The patient wasn't reassessed when they should have been. A worsening trend got overlooked. A message never got answered. A treatment plan kept running despite clear signs it wasn't working. Some safeguard that was supposed to catch this simply didn't fire. That instinct matters — it's usually what points toward the part of the record that deserves closer attention. But it isn't the analysis. The full picture still requires figuring out what the responsible professional actually knew at the time, what information they had access to, what authority they held, what a reasonable response would have looked like, and whether a different response probably would have changed what happened to this particular patient. Only after that does the attorney get to work out how that clinical picture fits into the governing law. Clinical Intelligence doesn't discourage a clinician from naming their concern. It just keeps that concern from getting presented as though every question downstream of it has already been answered — because a serious departure from good care and a serious injury can coexist in the same chart without one having caused the other. The reverse happens too: a fairly modest failure can meaningfully worsen an outcome even in a patient who already had significant disease going in. The work is connecting the conduct to what actually happened to this patient, not just noting that both a bad thing and a bad outcome occurred somewhere in the same record.

Medicine tends to think about outcomes as the product of many things happening at once. A patient might have advanced disease, limited physiological reserve, a treatment delay, medication effects, and a late complication, all contributing something to the final result — and a clinician is often perfectly comfortable saying that several factors played a role, without needing to rank them. The attorney doesn't get that luxury. Counsel has to work out how those factors relate to the actual legal claim: was the conduct in question the primary cause? Did it meaningfully worsen the injury? Did it speed up something that was already progressing? Did it take away the patient's chance at a better recovery? Did it create an entirely separate injury? Or, honestly, would the same outcome probably have happened anyway? Clinical Intelligence maps those relationships out before anyone tries to translate them into legal argument. It doesn't set the governing legal standard — that's not its job — but it gives the attorney and the retained experts a clearer clinical foundation to apply that standard against. That division protects both professions. The clinician never gets pulled into making a legal conclusion, and the attorney is never left trying to build causation out of language that was never precise enough to support it.

A shared language isn't really a glossary of agreed-upon definitions. It's closer to a common way of examining the case. Attorneys, clinicians, and experts should all be arriving at the same answers to a handful of fundamental questions, even while contributing very different expertise to answering them: can this evidence be trusted? Who was this patient before any of this happened? What actually occurred, and in what order? What do the objective findings and the imaging actually show? Which professional or which part of the healthcare system held responsibility at each point? When did the clinical picture start requiring a different response than the one it got? What treatment opportunity genuinely existed at that moment? What difference did the disputed care probably make? What other explanations have to be ruled out? And what, honestly, is still uncertain? Different people bring different expertise to those questions. What they shouldn't be doing is working from different versions of the patient.

A fair methodology has to be capable of landing in more than one place. It might show that the care was unreasonable and that the failure caused real harm. It might show that the care was reasonable despite a devastating outcome. It might find a genuine professional departure but conclude that the treatment window had already closed before anyone had the chance to act differently. It might reveal that one person got blamed for what was really a systems failure. It might show that pre-existing disease doesn't account for everything the patient lost afterward. It might narrow a case from complete prevention down to increased severity, or aggravation. It might conclude that more evidence is needed before anyone can say anything responsible. It might, sometimes, conclude that the case shouldn't go forward at all. What makes the method fair is that the same disciplined questions get applied no matter who's paying for the review. It doesn't promise a favorable answer. It promises a more reliable one — and that turns out to matter more than people expect, because credibility was never built by presenting only the supportive half of a case. It comes from showing that the difficult evidence got looked at honestly and the conclusion still held up anyway. Normal findings, temporary improvement, competing causes, pre-existing disease, reasonable professional judgment calls, the plain limits of what treatment can do — none of that needs to be hidden or waved away. It gets folded into the reasoning. A strong case doesn't get weaker when the contrary evidence is addressed honestly. It gets better prepared to survive being challenged.

I'd be doing this whole approach a disservice if I didn't admit that structure has its own risks. A detailed timeline can still be built on estimated times. A tidy diagram can make a genuinely complicated causal pathway look more certain than the underlying evidence actually supports. A classification label can end up carrying more weight in someone's judgment than the facts underneath it deserve. Technology, in particular, is very good at producing a coherent-looking account out of records that were incomplete, duplicated, or stitched together wrong. And there's a real risk that people start using the vocabulary of Clinical Intelligence without doing the reasoning underneath it — that baseline, treatment opportunity, record integrity, and causation mapping become labels dropped into a report rather than actual analysis. The method only works when every piece of it stays tethered to the patient and to the original source evidence. Clinical Intelligence is a tool. It was never meant to become an authority in its own right, and it only holds up when it stays grounded in professional boundaries, qualified expert review, honestly disclosed uncertainty, verified sources, and a human being's judgment at the end of it.

Let me give you an example of how this actually plays out. A sixty-eight-year-old comes into an emergency department with dizziness, vomiting, and trouble walking. The symptoms ease somewhat after treatment, and the patient is discharged. The next morning, they're back with weakness, and this time it's diagnosed as a posterior circulation stroke.

Read quickly, that's a straightforward sequence: discharged, then diagnosed with a major stroke the following day. It's easy to see how the first draft of the allegation becomes failure to diagnose the stroke.

The clinician reading the same chart sees more uncertainty sitting underneath that sequence. Dizziness and vomiting have a long list of possible causes. Feeling better after treatment can look reassuring in the moment. But the trouble walking deserves real scrutiny, depending on exactly how it was assessed, described, and documented at the time. The patient remembers not being able to walk safely. The record says the symptoms improved — but it never clearly shows that anyone reassessed the patient's gait before sending them home.

So the analysis starts, as it should, with figuring out what evidence actually exists. Maybe the full nursing assessment hasn't been produced yet. Maybe the original imaging is missing. Maybe prior records show this patient walking independently right up until this visit. Maybe the timeline shows the symptoms easing temporarily without ever showing that the functional problem — the unsteady gait — actually resolved.

Once you have that, the clinical question gets a lot more precise: was it reasonable to discharge a patient with vascular risk factors, ongoing difficulty walking, and a neurological reassessment that was never clearly documented? And the causal question stays separate from that, deliberately: would observation, more imaging, or an earlier neurological exam probably have changed the treatment or reduced how severe the stroke turned out to be?

One reading of that evidence says the unresolved gait problem needed further workup, and that catching it earlier probably would have reduced the resulting injury. Another reading says the initial presentation really was nonspecific, the rest of the exam was reassuring, the stroke simply progressed after the patient went home, or the patient wasn't a candidate for any intervention that would have changed the outcome regardless of when it was caught. The attorney, the clinician, and whatever experts get retained may still end up disagreeing about how strong this case actually is. But now they're disagreeing about the same questions, instead of talking past each other. That, in the end, is what a shared language buys you.

Law and medicine were never going to approach a case the exact same way, and they shouldn't. The attorney carries responsibilities the clinician doesn't have. The clinician carries knowledge the attorney was never trained to have. The goal isn't to make the two professions identical. It's to get them to a shared understanding: the clinician explaining what the evidence means medically, uncertainty and limitations included; the attorney working out how that meaning connects to legal responsibility, proof, causation, and strategy; the retained expert getting a focused question instead of a vague request to decide whether malpractice happened; everyone else on the case understanding how their piece fits into the larger journey the patient actually lived through.

There's one patient. There may be dozens of records, several professional vantage points on them, and more than one reasonable way to read what they say. Clinical Intelligence just lets those vantage points actually meet each other, without asking any single professional to give up their expertise, or reach past it.

Chapter Two: Why Law and Medicine See Different Cases

The same patient journey can turn into one story in medicine and an entirely different one in law, even when both professions are working honestly from the exact same record. The split starts with direction. Medicine looks forward. Law looks backward. And that single difference explains more of the friction in these cases than almost anything else.

The clinician is making decisions while the patient's condition is still unfolding, before anyone knows how it ends. The information in front of them may be incomplete, the symptoms may point in several directions at once, and the early findings may be normal or genuinely inconclusive. All they can do is assess the risk, decide what needs to happen right now, decide what can safely be watched instead, and stay ready to change course if the patient doesn't respond the way they expected.

By the time an attorney gets the case, all of that uncertainty has resolved into something known. The diagnosis is settled. The injury is visible, sometimes catastrophically so. Counsel is reading the record already knowing how it ends, and has to work out what could reasonably have been recognized earlier, whether the response at the time held up, whether a different response would have changed anything, and whether any of this can be turned into a legally supportable position.

Both of those approaches are doing exactly what they should. The tension between them is just built in. The clinician is asking what was reasonably knowable at the time. The attorney is asking what can now be shown about the decisions that were made. Clinical Intelligence exists because those two questions have to be connected to each other without letting hindsight quietly stand in for the uncertainty that was actually there while the care was happening.

Clinical care happens in real time, which is easy to say and surprisingly easy to forget once a case is sitting in a binder. A patient arrives with symptoms that could mean any number of things — some of them dangerous, most of them not. Early disease doesn't always announce itself with the findings you'd expect, and the patient rarely describes their symptoms in a way that makes the eventual diagnosis obvious in the moment. Nobody is expecting the clinician to land on the final diagnosis immediately. The first job is usually narrower: how dangerous does this look, what urgent possibilities need to be ruled out, what's a safe course of action right now, and is the plan something that can be revised if the patient doesn't improve the way it's supposed to.

That's a genuine exercise of judgment, made with limited time and incomplete information — results not back yet, a disease still evolving, a reasonable person having to act before certainty is even possible. None of that excuses bad care. But it is the actual condition under which the reasonableness of that care has to be judged, and forgetting it is the single easiest way to misjudge a medical case.

Legal review starts on the other side of all that, after the outcome is already known. The attorney is holding the file because something significant happened — permanent injury, lost function, extensive treatment, sometimes a death. Read backward from that outcome, the eventual diagnosis can look almost obvious. Counsel's job is to figure out whether the evidence actually supports a claim or a defense, which takes more than noticing that the result was bad. It means working out whether a duty existed, whether the conduct was unreasonable, whether a different response probably would have mattered, and what loss can honestly be tied to what happened.

Which means the legal process ends up asking questions in a form the treating clinician was never actually asking at the time. The clinician was deciding whether this patient needed admission; the attorney later asks whether discharging them was negligent. The clinician was weighing several possible diagnoses against each other; the attorney later asks why the real one got missed. The clinician was balancing the benefit of a treatment against its risk of bleeding, infection, or surgical complications;

the attorney later asks whether the choice they made is what caused the injury. There's nothing wrong with any of those legal questions. They only become unfair the moment the known outcome is allowed to rewrite what was actually knowable back when the decision was made.

Once a final diagnosis is on the table, everything that came before it starts to look sharper than it really was at the time. A patient who's later found to have a pulmonary embolism reported shortness of breath the day before — and suddenly that complaint reads like a screaming red flag. A patient later diagnosed with spinal cord compression complained of back pain and weakness, and in hindsight that combination looks unmistakable. A patient with a surgical leak had increasing pain and nausea, and now that sounds like it should have been obvious from the start. The later diagnosis is doing all of that retroactive sharpening. The real question is whether that meaning was actually available back when the symptom first showed up — whether it was isolated or part of a pattern that was already forming, whether there were objective findings that should have raised more concern, whether the patient got better in the meantime, whether the serious condition was reasonably on the list of possibilities being considered, whether the professional actually had enough information at that point to act differently.

It isn't enough to show that a symptom can now be linked, in hindsight, to the final diagnosis. The harder and more honest question is whether that link should reasonably have been made at the time, with the information that existed then. This is exactly where hindsight distorts a case — once you know how it ends, the earlier record can look like it was shouting a warning that, in reality, was faint, ambiguous, or genuinely easy to miss. Sometimes, to be fair, the warning really was clear and simply wasn't acted on. Telling those two situations apart is a large part of what Clinical Intelligence is for.

A disease can exist biologically well before it becomes something a clinician could reasonably identify, and that gap matters enormously in this kind of case. A tumor exists before it's reliably detectable. An infection is developing before it produces a pattern that demands escalation. A stroke is evolving before it throws off focal findings anyone would catch. Internal bleeding has already started before its symptoms become distinguishable from ordinary postoperative pain. The fact that a condition existed later doesn't prove it was diagnosable at every earlier point along the way — which is why the analysis has to pull apart biological presence, clinical presentation, reasonable recognizability, formal diagnosis, and treatment opportunity as separate, related stages rather than one collapsed moment. A condition can begin biologically while the symptoms are still too vague to diagnose, then become possible, then become reasonably recognizable, and only later get confirmed — with treatment remaining genuinely useful at one stage and no longer useful at another. Keeping those stages separate is what protects the analysis from hindsight, while still leaving room to identify a real missed opportunity where one actually existed.

Clinicians live inside provisional diagnoses more often than people outside medicine realize. A patient gets treated for the likeliest explanation while more serious possibilities are being considered or ruled out in the background, and the working diagnosis shifts as new evidence comes in. Someone looks dehydrated at first. Then a finding raises concern for infection. Then further deterioration reveals internal bleeding. The diagnosis changing over time doesn't automatically mean the earlier read was unreasonable. What actually matters is whether the clinician stayed responsive to the evidence as it developed — was the original explanation reasonable given what was known when it was made, what findings should have challenged it, did the patient improve the way that explanation predicted, were abnormal results actually acknowledged, was the plan revised once the course stopped matching the story. A working diagnosis was never a promise that the first conclusion would hold. It's a position that has to stay open to being revised, which is exactly why reassessment carries so much weight in these cases — a perfectly reasonable initial call can turn unreasonable the moment someone keeps leaning on it after the patient's condition has clearly moved on.

Litigation, though, can't live forever in a fog of several medical possibilities. At some point counsel has to commit to a theory — a complaint, an expert disclosure, a demand, a mediation position, a defense all require a clear account of what's being alleged and why the evidence supports it. That creates real tension between clinical uncertainty and the clarity litigation demands. The answer isn't to force the medicine into a certainty it doesn't have. It's to find the strongest claim the evidence can honestly carry. Maybe the evidence never supports that a stroke should have been caught at the first mention of dizziness — but it does support that persistent trouble walking needed a further look before discharge. Maybe it never shows that a postoperative complication was avoidable — but it does show that the patient's deterioration needed to be recognized and rescued sooner than it was. Tying the clinical question to the actual decision point, instead of the broadest possible description of the event, tends to make the theory more useful, not less. A precise theory usually isn't a weaker one. Often it's stronger, precisely because it's built out of what the evidence can actually prove.

Clinicians and attorneys also just weigh different evidence differently. A clinician tends to lean on trends, functional change, how the patient responded to treatment, subtle deterioration, the relationship among several findings taken together — the significance often lives in the pattern, not in any single entry. An attorney leans harder on documentation, contradictions, policies, admissions, testimony, whatever can actually be proven with admissible evidence. Both kinds of attention matter. A clinician might recognize that a falling blood pressure paired with a rising heart rate is medically alarming even though no note ever uses the word "unstable" — and the attorney still has to work out how to establish and present that finding to someone who isn't a clinician. An attorney might spot a contradiction between testimony and the chart, and the clinician has to explain whether that contradiction actually changes the medical picture or is really just a detail with no bearing on what happened to the patient. The most medically important fact in a case isn't always the easiest one to prove. The most obvious contradiction on the page isn't always the one that actually moves the case.

A gap in the record gets read differently by each profession, too. An attorney tends to treat a missing note as evidence that an assessment, a conversation, an intervention simply didn't happen. A clinician knows perfectly well that plenty of real care never makes it fully into the chart. Neither reading should be automatic. The honest approach asks whether the event would ordinarily have been documented at all, how significant the event actually was, whether other entries reference it indirectly, whether testimony supports it, whether an audit trail exists somewhere, and whether its absence changes the clinical picture in any meaningful way. There's a real difference between saying something wasn't documented and saying it didn't happen — the first is a description of the record, the second is a conclusion about the event, and the evidence has to earn that extra step. A missing routine vital sign might not move the needle at all. A missing neurological reassessment before discharge might be the whole case. Context decides which one you're looking at.

A normal result can look almost conclusive once a case is being reviewed legally, and clinically it's often much narrower than that. A normal lab value doesn't rule out early disease. A normal exam only reflects what was actually tested and written down. A normal scan may simply have missed something too early, too small, outside what that particular study was sensitive to, or outside the area it even looked at. None of that means normal findings should be waved off — plenty of the time, they're strong evidence that a condition genuinely wasn't recognizable, or wasn't there yet. The real question is what that result could reasonably establish, which means asking not just whether it came back normal but whether it actually answered the clinical question that mattered at the time. A test can be normal and still be the wrong test to rule out the thing everyone was worried about. It can also be exactly the right test, and strong support for the decision that got made. Which one you're looking at depends on the timing, the study performed, the symptoms in front of the clinician, the known limits of that test, and everything else that happened afterward.

Improvement gets misread just as often. One reader sees the symptoms improve and takes that as support for sending the patient home. Another sees the later deterioration and decides the improvement must have been misleading all along. The clinician's question is narrower and more useful: what improved, why did it improve, and was that improvement enough to make the plan actually safe? Pain can ease with medication while the underlying problem hasn't changed at all. Oxygen levels can look better because support was turned up. Blood pressure can rise briefly after fluids while internal bleeding continues underneath. Nausea can settle while weakness or a neurological problem is still very much there. One symptom getting better doesn't mean the clinical problem resolved — you have to look at the whole picture together: function, vital signs, the exam, lab trends, how much support the patient still needed. Improvement that's temporary, partial, or entirely dependent on ongoing treatment means something different from actual recovery, and mixing the two up is one of the more common ways these cases go sideways.

Medicine often has to respond to risk before there's any certainty behind it. A patient might not have a confirmed diagnosis and still carry enough risk to justify monitoring, more testing, a consult, or at least a more cautious discharge plan. Law, later, asks whether that risk created an actual obligation — and the answer depends on how serious the possible condition was, how likely it seemed at the time, what evidence supported the worry, what further steps were realistically available, and how burdensome or risky those steps would have been. Not every conceivable possibility demands the most aggressive response; medicine would grind to a halt if it did. But some risks genuinely can't be waved off, and part of Clinical Intelligence is figuring out the point where the uncertainty itself became the thing requiring action — where the question stops being "was the diagnosis known" and becomes "was the unresolved risk too significant to let the existing plan just keep running."

A great many medical cases, when you really get into them, aren't about the first decision at all. They're about the failure to ever revisit it. An initial plan can be entirely reasonable — the patient looked low risk, the testing was reassuring, the likely diagnosis was benign — and then the patient doesn't improve, or a new symptom shows up, or a lab trend worsens, or a family member reports something has clearly changed, or the treatment simply isn't doing what it's supposed to. That's the moment the professional obligation can shift, and it's exactly why the patient's whole journey matters so much more than any single note in isolation. The real question is whether the care stayed responsive as the evidence changed — which means judging the initial call separately from whatever failure came later to reconsider it. Keeping those two things apart tends to produce a fairer and more accurate theory of the case: one that doesn't condemn a perfectly reasonable first decision, while still naming the exact point where continuing to lean on that decision stopped being safe.

Attorneys, understandably, tend to start with whatever event was most visible to the client. The patient was discharged and got worse — so the case becomes "wrongful discharge." A surgical complication happened — so the operation becomes the focus. The diagnosis came late — so every earlier visit gets treated as a missed diagnosis. Working through the case honestly can reveal that the stronger issue is sitting somewhere else entirely. The discharge might have been perfectly reasonable, but a later phone call should have triggered urgent reassessment and didn't. The surgical complication itself might have been unavoidable, while the response to the patient's deterioration afterward was too slow. The first visit might genuinely have been ambiguous, while the second one had clear warning signs that got missed. Moving the theory when that happens isn't inconsistency — it's what's supposed to happen once the evidence gets clearer. The whole point of the review was never to defend the first allegation at all costs. It's to find the theory that actually reflects what happened to the patient, and a theory should move when the evidence moves.

Sometimes an attorney and a clinician look like they're disagreeing when they're actually both right about different parts of the same case. The clinician might be right that the initial symptom really was nonspecific. The attorney might be right that the chart never showed a required assessment being done. The clinician might be right that the ultimate outcome wasn't preventable. The attorney might be right that a delay still made the injury worse than it needed to be. An expert might be right that two different treatment approaches were both medically acceptable — and the hospital might still have failed to make sure either one was actually carried out safely. None of this requires picking a winner between the two perspectives. It just requires figuring out how they fit together. A single case can hold reasonable care at one stage and unreasonable care at the next. It can hold an unavoidable condition alongside preventable additional harm. It can hold an entirely sound clinical judgment that a systems failure then prevented anyone from actually carrying out. The patient's journey can contain more than one truth at the same time, and a good review has to be able to hold all of them.

Attorneys sometimes defer too much to clinicians, simply because the subject matter feels technical and out of their depth. A clinician says the complication was unavoidable, or that the care was reasonable, and counsel accepts it without ever really understanding the reasoning underneath. Professional authority does matter here — but it shouldn't stand in for analysis. The attorney should still be able to ask what evidence actually supports that opinion, what alternatives were considered, which part of the outcome was truly unavoidable, whether the early care was fine but the later response wasn't, and whether the expert's specialty even covers the specific issue in question. None of that turns the attorney into a clinician. It just gives counsel enough structure to ask informed questions instead of nodding along — and it cuts both ways: the attorney shouldn't substitute their own medical judgment for a qualified opinion, but they also shouldn't accept a conclusion that can't be explained, tested, or tied back to the actual evidence.

Clinicians, for their part, sometimes misjudge what an attorney actually needs from them. A careful clinical write-up can walk through several possibilities thoughtfully and never actually say which interpretation is better supported. It can identify an error without ever addressing whether that error affected the outcome. It can describe the medicine accurately and still leave the attorney with no idea what to do next. The clinician was never being asked to make the legal call. But they do need to communicate the clinical findings in a way that lets someone else make that call. A shared language should hold onto medical complexity without leaving the whole analysis directionless — uncertainty deserves to be explained honestly, but it shouldn't become an excuse to avoid naming the most supportable conclusion. When several readings remain genuinely possible, the useful thing a clinician can do is say which one the evidence favors, what supports it, what limits it, and which parts genuinely need a specialist's opinion. That's both clinically honest and legally useful, which is a combination worth aiming for every time.

There's also a quieter risk worth naming: once someone has committed to a theory, the way they read the record can start drifting toward that theory almost without noticing. Supportive evidence gets more attention. Contrary evidence gets treated as a footnote instead of something to reason through. Language that started out ambiguous gets more confident every time it's repeated in a demand, a brief, a presentation. This happens on both sides of a case — a plaintiff's theory can grow past what the evidence actually supports, and a defense read can just as easily minimize a real failure because something else also contributed to the outcome. Part of what this whole approach is supposed to do is interrupt that drift. When the evidence genuinely supports a strong conclusion, it should say so plainly. When it only supports something narrower, the language needs to narrow right along with it. The credibility of any review comes down to whether it's willing to preserve what the evidence actually means, even when that meaning doesn't line up perfectly with whichever side is paying for the analysis.

A review earns credibility precisely by letting the reader see that the evidence was tested, not curated. That means naming the uncertainty, the normal findings, the temporary improvement, the competing causes, the pre-existing disease, the patient's own choices, the honest limits of treatment, the reasonable judgment calls — none of which automatically weakens a case that's actually supportable. If anything, it shows the conclusion survived contact with the hardest evidence rather than being built by avoiding it. The same principle runs the other way for a defense review: genuine process failures, inconsistent charting, missed escalation shouldn't get minimized just because something else was also going on. A conclusion that's already survived a balanced look at the evidence is simply worth more than one built by only emphasizing the parts that support the outcome someone was hoping for.

When law and medicine are actually working from the same structured understanding of a case, a lot of things get better at once. The attorney lands on the right question sooner. The clinician can explain the medical significance of something without drifting into a legal conclusion they're not equipped to make. The retained expert gets a focused assignment instead of a vague one. Discovery starts following the unresolved question instead of just the size of the record. The client gets a more honest account of where the case is strong and where it isn't. Most importantly, the legal theory stays tied to the patient rather than to whichever document happens to be on top. The result of all that isn't always agreement — it's usually a much better-defined disagreement, and decisions that are made more responsibly because of it. Law and medicine are always going to carry different responsibilities, different standards, different ways of reasoning, and a shared framework was never meant to pretend every clinical uncertainty converts neatly into a legal answer. Its job isn't to erase the differences between the two professions. It's to make those differences visible enough, and understandable enough, to actually be useful.

Here's how this plays out in practice. A forty-three-year-old has laparoscopic surgery and goes home the same day. Over the next two days they report worsening abdominal pain, nausea, weakness, and trouble keeping fluids down. The surgical office tells them to hydrate, take pain medication, and keep watching it. They eventually end up in the emergency department with sepsis from a bowel injury.

Read quickly, that looks like a surgical error followed by a delayed diagnosis — surgery, injury, deterioration, sepsis, in a neat line. A surgeon looking at the same chart may see something different: a recognized complication that isn't necessarily something anyone could have seen during the operation, layered on top of postoperative pain and nausea that are, to some degree, expected in early recovery.

Both readings can be partly true at once. One question is whether the bowel injury itself resulted from unreasonable surgical technique — which needs proper surgical review to answer. A separate question is whether the postoperative course became concerning enough that it should have triggered an earlier in-person assessment. The records might show pain that was climbing rather than easing, weakness setting in, oral intake becoming difficult — while the office's own documentation of the phone calls is thin, and doesn't clearly establish what was actually reported.

One honest reading of that evidence says the developing pattern called for an in-person look before the patient became septic, and that earlier treatment probably would have reduced how sick they got. Another honest reading says the symptoms as reported stayed within an expected range right up until a sudden later change. The surgical technique could have been entirely reasonable even if the postoperative response to it wasn't. The bowel injury itself might have been unavoidable even while some of what followed was preventable. Law and medicine looked like they were seeing two different cases here mostly because each one started with a different question — and working through it carefully shows that this case may actually contain two separate issues, needing separate evidence and possibly separate experts to resolve.

If I had to boil all of this down to one question that both professions could genuinely share, it would be something like: what was reasonably knowable, what did that information call for, and what difference would a different response probably have made? That single question pulls together the evidence, the patient's baseline, the timeline, the clinical meaning of the findings, who held responsibility, what treatment opportunity existed, what else might explain the outcome, and why any of it matters legally. The attorney and the clinician will bring different pieces of the answer. What matters is that they're answering the same question.

Law and medicine see different cases because they walk into the same patient's journey from opposite directions — medicine deciding before the outcome is known, law evaluating after it's already clear. The clinician's job is explaining what was actually knowable at the time. The attorney's job is working out what that understanding means under the law. Clinical Intelligence connects those two without asking either profession to set aside its own judgment. It protects the case from hindsight, while making sure genuine uncertainty never becomes an excuse for failing to respond once a patient's condition had plainly changed. None of this is about getting law to think like medicine, or medicine to think like law. It's about getting both of them to understand the same journey before anyone decides what it means.

Chapter Three: How the Patient Gets Lost in the Record

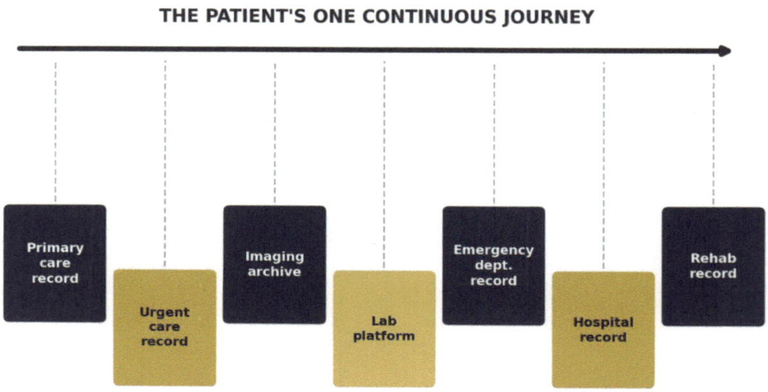

Each system holds one piece. No single record holds the whole story.

Figure 3.1 — One journey, many records

A patient's story almost never shows up in one place. That sounds obvious once you say it out loud, and it's still one of the main reasons medical cases get misunderstood by people reading them for the first time.

The patient lived through one continuous experience — got sick, sought help, talked to different people, went through tests, got treated, improved, got worse, came back, got transferred, or went home with questions nobody ever answered. To them, every one of those moments belonged to the same unbroken journey. The medical record was never built to follow that experience the same way. It splits the journey up by profession, department, facility, software system, and purpose. A physician documents one slice of it. A nurse documents another.

Medications live somewhere else. Imaging often sits in an entirely separate archive that hasn't even been produced yet.

A phone call gets reduced to two lines. A lab result shows up in the chart without any indication of who actually received it, who understood what it meant, or who was supposed to act on it. By the time all of this reaches your desk, the patient's experience has often been chopped into so many separate pieces that it barely resembles the story they actually lived through. This is where an attorney can find themselves at a real disadvantage without even realizing it — sitting on thousands of pages and still missing the piece of evidence that would actually explain the case. The problem, more often than not, isn't that there's too little information. It's that nobody has connected what's already there.

Medical records get created for a whole range of reasons that have nothing to do with someone eventually reviewing them in litigation — supporting the care itself, letting professionals communicate with each other, documenting observations and decisions, recording orders and treatment, satisfying billing requirements, demonstrating compliance with whatever the institution requires. Nobody writing a note in the moment is drafting a complete explanation for a future lawyer. They're documenting within the immediate needs of the unit they're standing in, not preparing a retrospective account of every fact that might someday matter.

A physician might record the conclusion without ever writing down the full reasoning that led there. A nurse might describe a change in the patient without saying whether that change actually altered the medical plan. A lab result can appear in the chart with no indication of whether the responsible physician ever saw it, or understood what it required of them. A discharge summary might describe the diagnosis and outcome cleanly while saying almost nothing about the hours when the patient's condition was actually shifting underneath everyone. A phone note might confirm that a call happened without capturing the words the patient actually used, how urgent it sounded, or what advice was actually given.

None of that makes the record useless, or inherently unreliable. It just means you have to understand what each piece of it was created to show, and what it simply can't establish on its own. One note tells you what was observed. Another tells you what was ordered. A third tells you whether that order was actually carried out. A later entry might tell you whether the patient responded — and only once you've pulled all of those threads together does the care start to look anything like the journey the patient actually lived through.

Picture a patient who starts with a phone call to primary care, then goes to urgent care, gets tested through an outside lab, goes home, worsens overnight, ends up in an emergency department, gets transferred to another hospital, has surgery, moves into rehab, and eventually receives care at home. That's one patient's journey. The evidence of it might be scattered across six or seven completely separate systems, each of which only ever saw its own slice of the whole thing. Primary care holds the first report of symptoms. Urgent care holds the exam, while the lab results come back through an external interface after the patient has already left. The emergency department might reference the prior visit briefly without holding the complete record of it. The receiving hospital documents the condition as it looked after significant deterioration had already set in. Rehab records often end up holding the clearest account of what the patient actually lost, functionally. Home-health notes can reveal needs that never made it into the acute hospital chart at all.

Every one of those records starts and stops at a different point, and every organization tends to treat its own slice as a complete encounter — even though the patient never experienced a series of disconnected encounters. They experienced one condition, developing over time. Reviewed separately, the significance of any single event can become almost invisible. A symptom noted in primary care might only matter once you place it next to a lab result that came back weeks later. An outside image might explain a "sudden" deterioration that only looks sudden because the hospital never saw what came before it. A family phone call might reveal that the patient's condition had already changed hours before the next formal assessment. No single source necessarily holds the whole truth. Put together, they can reveal a course of events that's a good deal more accurate than any one of them looked alone.

A thick production can create a false sense of security all on its own. When a file runs to several thousand pages, it's tempting to assume everything important must already be sitting in there somewhere. Volume and completeness are not the same thing. A large production can be padded with hundreds of duplicate pages, repeated medication lists, billing records, templated instructions, copied histories — an impressive page count that still manages to be missing the original imaging, a critical nursing flowsheet, a medication-administration record, a lab-routing log, or a transfer-center file. The real question was never just "have the medical records been produced." It's "has the evidence needed to answer this particular question actually been produced." A preliminary screening might not need every available source — there may be enough already in hand to decide the concern is clinically plausible and worth digging into further. A final opinion about delayed recognition, though, might need a great deal more: precise timing, the exact route information traveled through, the original diagnostic images, whether the patient was even eligible for the treatment in question, the point where a different response could still have changed the outcome. A damages analysis might need years of baseline records, functional assessments, rehab documentation, employment history, later care. An institutional question might need policies, staffing records, audit histories, communication logs — evidence that never appears in the ordinary patient chart at all. What counts as "complete" depends entirely on the question being asked. A record can be plenty for one decision and hopelessly inadequate for another.

Time itself turns out to be more complicated than it looks on the page. A chart is full of different times, and they don't all describe the same event. There's the time something happened, and the time someone noticed it. There's the time an entry was started, the time it was finished, the time it was signed. There's the time a test was ordered, the time it was actually performed, the time the result became available, the time someone reviewed it, and the time anyone acted on it. Those gaps can be the whole case. A note signed at four in the afternoon might be describing a conversation that happened at noon. A medication ordered at two might not have actually been given until three-thirty. A significant lab result might have hit the electronic chart at nine in the morning and just sat in a queue until someone finally opened it hours later.

Treat all of those times as though they mean the same thing, and you risk building the case around the wrong delay entirely — assuming a professional knew something the moment it entered the system, when all the evidence actually shows is that the information was technically available somewhere. The opposite mistake happens too: a note entered hours late can make it look like an event happened later than it really did, when the conversation itself was prompt and only the paperwork lagged behind. This is exactly why a meaningful timeline can't just copy dates and times straight out of the chart — it has to identify what each one of those times actually represents. The question worth asking usually isn't when a result technically existed. It's when that result became available to the person responsible for it, when it should reasonably have been reviewed, and when the need to act on it became clear. Those are three different points along the same journey, and mixing them up changes the whole shape of the case.

The same statement showing up in several notes can look, at first glance, like independent confirmation from multiple professionals. Often it's just copied language. A phrase like "alert and oriented," "no acute distress," or "stable" gets carried forward from one note into the next. A diagnosis stays on the problem list long after its relevance has changed. A normal finding keeps appearing even when nothing suggests the exam was actually repeated. None of that necessarily means the information is wrong — it means repetition shouldn't be mistaken for separate observation unless the record actually supports that someone looked again. Five notes repeating the same phrase aren't always five independent findings. Sometimes they're one finding, wearing five different timestamps. That distinction can genuinely change how a case reads: documentation repeating that a patient was neurologically intact can look persuasive right up until it becomes clear the language traces back to a single earlier assessment, copied forward without anyone actually re-examining the patient. Histories and symptom descriptions run into the same problem — an initial account can echo through several later notes, creating an illusion of consistency that's really just several professionals relying on the same original source. None of this means copied language is automatically inaccurate. It just means the honest question is whether a given phrase reflects a new observation, a repeated conclusion, or something carried forward out of convenience — because only once you know which one you're looking at can you give it the weight it deserves.

Discharge and transfer summaries are genuinely useful — they pull a huge amount of information together and give you a clean overview of the final diagnosis, the major treatment, the outcome. They also compress the story, almost by design. A summary usually gets written after the important events are already known, which means it tends to explain what was ultimately diagnosed and how the patient was treated while giving very little space to the stretch of time when the patient was actually deteriorating and the diagnosis was still unclear. A discharge summary might state plainly that the patient developed sepsis and needed intensive care, without ever showing the preceding hours of falling blood pressure, worsening confusion, dropping urine output, and climbing oxygen requirements. A later summary might state that the patient had a stroke, without ever addressing whether gait was assessed at the earlier visit, whether the symptoms genuinely resolved, or whether temporary improvement got mistaken for actual recovery. The single most important stretch of the whole case can end up missing from the summary entirely — sitting instead in a nursing flowsheet, a medication record, a phone log, the original imaging, or a scattering of small changes spread across several separate notes. A summary should guide the review. It shouldn't control it. It tells you how the person writing it, after the fact, made sense of the course of events — it doesn't replace the evidence that was actually created while those events were still unfolding. Very often, the moment that matters most in the whole case is exactly the moment the summary glides past the fastest.

One of the easiest mistakes to make in reviewing a medical record is assuming that an order proves the thing actually happened. It doesn't. A medication can be ordered and never given. A consult can be requested and never completed. A scan can be ordered and then delayed for days. A transfer can be initiated and never accepted anywhere. A lab test can be requested and never actually collected. A treatment can sit right there in the plan with no evidence it ever reached the patient. The gap between a decision and its implementation matters enormously, because responsibility can shift in that gap — the clinician may have made exactly the right call, and the system around them may simply have failed to carry it out. A delay might trace back to a missed order, a short-staffed department, a patient who wasn't available, a receiving hospital with no open bed, or a plan that changed later for good reason. Each of those explanations means something different. A case can look, at first glance, like an individual clinical failure when the real problem actually occurred later, somewhere in the process of carrying out the plan. It can just as easily look like a systems failure when the delay actually has a perfectly reasonable explanation that simply isn't visible on a first pass. The journey has to be traced all the way from decision to action. Knowing a scan was ordered isn't enough — you need to know when it was scheduled, when it was actually performed, when the result came back, who received it, and what happened next. The same discipline applies to medication, consults, transfers, escalation of any kind. Clinical care lives in what actually got carried out, not merely in what someone wrote down as the plan.

Records often tell you what treatment was given without telling you what happened afterward. A patient gets fluids, antibiotics, pain medication, oxygen, whatever the situation calls for — and that tells you what was done, not whether it worked. Pain can ease while the underlying condition keeps getting worse underneath it. Blood pressure can rise briefly after fluids and then start falling again. Oxygen levels can look better simply because support was increased, not because the patient actually improved. Nausea can settle while weakness lingers. A fever can break with medication while the infection driving it keeps progressing regardless. The patient's response to treatment is very often exactly where the need for reassessment first becomes visible — if the intervention produced the improvement everyone expected, sticking with the original plan may have been entirely reasonable. When the patient doesn't respond that way, the whole meaning of the case shifts. The original explanation may no longer fit what's actually happening, and a decision that was reasonable when it was made may need to be revisited. Treatment should never really be looked at as a standalone event — the analysis has to connect what was given to what happened next. A chart that records the medication without recording the response is only telling you half the story.

Some of the most important evidence in a medical case doesn't live in the ordinary chart at all. It shows up in audit trails, phone systems, patient portal messages, lab-routing platforms, transfer-center records, pharmacy systems, staffing records, device data, original imaging — sources that can show who had access to information, when a message got assigned to someone, when a result got acknowledged, whether a transfer was delayed, or whether treatment happened when the main chart merely implies that it did. This matters most in cases that turn on communication. The chart shows the abnormal result. It doesn't necessarily show the route that result was supposed to travel, who was responsible for watching the queue it landed in, whether a notification actually fired, or whether anyone ever opened it. The medical record might say the physician was informed. The phone log might show that no call was ever completed, while the audit history shows the physician accessed the result through a completely different route. A transfer note might say arrangements were being made. The transfer-center record might show that several facilities turned the patient down, that no bed existed anywhere nearby, or that the request wasn't even placed until much later than anyone assumed. The failure, in cases like these, often stays invisible until you actually reconstruct the information pathway itself — and doing that can shift the whole focus of the case. What looked like one professional's failure can turn out to be a system that never reliably routed information in the first place. What looked like an institutional failure can turn out to be a perfectly reasonable process that simply ran into an external limitation nobody inside the hospital could control. The evidence has to be allowed to show you where responsibility actually sat.

Patients speak in ordinary language, and medical records translate that language into clinical terms — sometimes faithfully, sometimes with real meaning lost along the way. A patient says, "I couldn't stand up," and the note says dizziness. They say, "I couldn't catch my breath," and the note says shortness of breath. A patient who says "I felt like something was terribly wrong" might get written up as anxious. That translation can be reasonable and still strip out the very part of the story that mattered most. Function tends to be far more revealing than whatever label got chosen for it: could the patient walk safely, keep fluids down, stay awake, take care of themselves, do the things they could manage just fine before all of this started? Those questions often explain the clinical change more clearly than any diagnosis list or clinical shorthand ever could. None of this means the patient's account should be taken at face value simply because it's personal — memory bends under time, distress, later information, and the sheer weight of a serious outcome. It also shouldn't be waved off just because it wasn't phrased in medical language. It's another piece of evidence, to be weighed against the contemporaneous record, family observations, functional findings, and everything that happened afterward. Sometimes the patient's own words are exactly what explains what the medical shorthand quietly left out.

There's a natural pull toward filling in an incomplete story. When the record has an unexplained gap, it's tempting to just infer what probably happened — a clinician assumes a routine assessment must have occurred, an attorney assumes the missing documentation means it didn't. Either assumption can carry the analysis further than the evidence actually supports. A missing assessment is a missing assessment, unless some other source establishes that it happened. A missing conversation stays unproven unless testimony, audit data, a phone record, or another entry backs it up. The same discipline has to apply to the patient's own recollection — a later account can be genuinely important evidence, but it shouldn't quietly replace contemporaneous documentation that was never there to begin with. None of this means every gap has to be resolved. Some cases stay genuinely incomplete, and that uncertainty itself can determine how far a case can responsibly go. The goal was never a seamless narrative at any cost. It's knowing what's actually established, what's reasonably inferred, what's disputed, and what's simply missing. An honest gap tells you more than a confident guess ever will.

A detailed chronology can list every single date and still fail to explain the case. It can tell you when the patient showed up, when the test was ordered, when the medication was given, when the diagnosis was finally made — and never once tell you when the meaning of the patient's condition actually changed. That's the whole difference: interpretation. A chronology shows pain medication given at two and imaging done at six. The patient's journey asks whether the medication actually worked, whether the symptoms came back, what prompted the decision to finally get imaging, and whether that four-hour gap held a real treatment opportunity inside it. A chronology shows blood pressure dropping over the course of an evening. The journey asks whether that drop actually represented deterioration for this particular patient, whether other findings were shifting at the same time, who got told, and what response the moment actually called for. The chronology puts events in order. The journey explains why any of those events mattered in the first place — which is exactly where Clinical Intelligence goes further than simply organizing a record. It reconstructs the clinical meaning of the course, without pretending every question can be answered from the chart alone.

Let me walk through how this plays out. A seventy-six-year-old woman lives independently despite several chronic conditions. Over a few days she develops fatigue, poor appetite, and intermittent confusion. She goes to primary care, then to an urgent-care center, where labs get ordered. A significant abnormal result comes back the next day. Several days after that, she's admitted to the hospital with a severe infection and organ dysfunction.

Her family believes the result was simply ignored. A first pass through the chart seems to support that — the abnormal result is sitting right there, and there's no clear follow-up note before the hospital admission. The wider record tells a more complicated story. The test was ordered through one service and came back through an external lab interface. It landed in a shared electronic queue, and a notification went out through the patient portal — though nothing shows she ever opened it. The urgent-care record also shows she'd been told to go to the emergency department if things got worse. Her earlier records confirm she'd been living independently, but they also document chronic kidney disease, which may well have affected both how that lab result should have been read and how quickly she deteriorated afterward.

At that point, the case can't be reduced to "an abnormal result sat there with no follow-up." What actually needs answering is how that queue was supposed to be monitored, who was responsible for reviewing the result, whether it was classified correctly in the first place, and whether any further notification should have gone out. It needs to be established whether her symptoms had already become serious enough to need emergency evaluation on their own, and whether the advice she'd been given was clear enough to act on. And then there's the causal question sitting underneath all of it: would direct contact on the day the result came back have led to earlier treatment? Was her infection already far enough along that the eventual outcome couldn't have been prevented entirely regardless? Could earlier intervention plausibly have reduced how sick she got, even if some hospitalization was always going to be necessary? Did she actually understand the return-precaution advice, and was she capable of acting on it while intermittently confused?

One honest reading of all that shows a system that failed to make sure a significant result actually reached the person responsible for it, and the patient herself — and that earlier contact probably would have led to treatment before organ dysfunction ever set in. Another honest reading shows a result that wasn't specific enough to demand immediate action, appropriate return precautions that were given clearly, and a condition that deteriorated later despite a perfectly reasonable initial plan. The review might ultimately land on individual responsibility, systemic responsibility, some mix of both, or no actionable failure at all — and none of that can be decided just from the fact that an abnormal result exists somewhere in the file. The patient's journey has to be pieced back together across the clinical record, the lab interface, the communication systems, her prior baseline, and the hospital course that followed. Only then does the case actually come into focus.

The patient lived one story. The record split it into pieces. The job was never just to gather those pieces up or line them up by date. It's understanding how they connect, where they contradict each other, what's missing, and what all of it together says about the patient's changing condition and the care they received. That means looking past whatever note is most visible on the surface — telling an order apart from its implementation, a timestamp apart from the event it supposedly represents, repeated language apart from an actual independent observation, a tidy clinical summary apart from the messy period of uncertainty it quietly compressed. It also means listening carefully to the patient's own account, without treating it as either gospel or noise — because the patient's voice belongs inside the evidence, especially when it explains a functional change that the clinical shorthand simply failed to capture. Reconstructing the journey was never about making a case sound more persuasive. It's about making it more accurate. That accuracy might strengthen the original theory. It might shift responsibility from one professional to another, expose a systems failure, narrow the alleged delay, or reveal that the evidence simply can't carry the first assumption anyone made about it. A case doesn't become clear because the record is thick. It becomes clear the moment the patient's actual journey can finally be seen inside it.

Chapter Four: When Clinical Meaning Changes in Translation

The trouble between law and medicine isn't always that facts are missing. More often, the facts are all there, and what changes is their meaning, as it passes from one professional to the next. A clinician writes something down. Another clinician interprets it. A reviewer summarizes it. An attorney builds a legal theory on top of that summary, and eventually an expert gets asked to respond to that theory. By the time any of this reaches mediation, a deposition, or a courtroom, the original clinical meaning can have quietly become broader, narrower, or more certain than the underlying evidence ever actually supported.

That drift rarely happens because someone was careless. Usually every professional along the way is just trying to make the information useful inside their own role. The clinician speaks the language of risk, uncertainty, response, possibility. The attorney eventually has to speak the language of responsibility, proof, causation, damages. The problem shows up in the gap between those two languages — in what gets lost, or added, in the translation. Keeping that meaning intact across the whole handoff is really the whole task. It's less about giving law and medicine a shared vocabulary than giving them a way to translate the evidence without quietly changing what it says.

Medical records are full of words that look completely ordinary and easy to understand. Stable, normal, improved, significant, possible, likely, preventable, unavoidable — none of them look like technical language. And yet every one of them can carry a clinical meaning that differs from whatever meaning an attorney, a client, or a jury would naturally give it. That's actually what makes familiar words more dangerous than unfamiliar ones. A genuinely technical term tends to prompt a question.

An ordinary word slides right past everyone, because everyone assumes they already understand it.

Take the word stable. To an attorney, it can sound like the patient was doing fine, wasn't in danger, had improved enough that the existing plan made sense. Clinically, it can mean nothing more than that the patient wasn't changing rapidly at that particular moment. They might have remained critically ill, dependent on escalating support, at serious risk of decline — and still counted as "stable" the whole time. A patient can be stable on a ventilator. Stable while on medication just to keep their blood pressure up. Stable because oxygen was increased. The word doesn't tell you the patient was well. It tells you that one part of their condition wasn't visibly shifting during whatever window is being described. The meaning has to come from everything around it.

This becomes especially important once a record gets reviewed after a sudden decline. Say a patient is described as stable for hours before things suddenly fall apart. The repeated use of that word can look, on its face, like support for the idea that the change was unexpected and couldn't reasonably have been caught sooner. That reading might be correct. It might also be missing half the picture. Vital signs can sit inside an acceptable range while mental status, mobility, urine output, respiratory effort, or alertness quietly gets worse the whole time. A note can call a patient stable because blood pressure and heart rate haven't moved, even as that same patient grows steadily more confused. So the word has to be tied to whatever it's actually describing — was this patient hemodynamically stable, neurologically stable, or just unchanged from the last time someone looked? Was that stability happening on its own, or was it propped up by treatment and support the whole time? A word that sounds reassuring can hide exactly the change that mattered, if you read it without the context underneath it.

Improvement runs into the same problem. A patient reporting less pain after medication is, technically, an improvement — it just doesn't tell you the underlying condition got any better. Nausea can settle while the pathology causing it keeps progressing. Oxygen saturation can rise simply because more oxygen was given. Blood pressure can look better briefly after fluids while bleeding continues underneath it the whole time. So the honest question is what improved, how long it lasted, and whether the change actually addressed the problem that created the risk in the first place. A patient who came in with dizziness and trouble walking might report less nausea after treatment — but if nobody reassessed their gait, the record simply can't establish that the functional problem that actually mattered ever resolved. A postoperative patient might report less pain on medication while getting weaker and unable to keep fluids down — and that drop in pain shouldn't be allowed to speak for the whole clinical picture. Improvement only means something once you know exactly what changed, and what didn't.

Normal results have the same slipperiness once they're pulled out of their clinical setting. A normal test can be strong evidence that a condition wasn't present, or wasn't yet recognizable. It can also carry very little weight, depending on which test was run, how far the disease had progressed, the quality of the study, or what condition was even being considered in the first place. The real question was never just whether the result came back normal. It's what that result was actually capable of ruling out. A normal early lab value might not rule out an infection that's still developing. A normal neurological exam only reflects whatever functions someone actually tested and wrote down. A normal scan might simply have missed something too early, too small, outside what that modality can detect, or outside the area it was even looking at. None of this is license to dismiss normal findings whenever they're inconvenient — a genuinely appropriate, genuinely normal study can be strong support for exactly the decision that got made. What matters is the meaning of the result, not the label sitting next to it.

Few words cause more trouble between law and medicine than possible. Clinicians reach for it constantly, because medicine so often requires holding several explanations in mind at once. A disease can be possible without being the leading suspect. A treatment can possibly help without anyone being confident about how much. A complication can possibly have contributed without being anywhere close to the primary cause. Litigation, by contrast, usually needs more definition than that. When a clinician says earlier treatment could have helped, the attorney has to figure out whether that's describing biological possibility or an actual probable difference in outcome — because those are not the same opinion wearing different words. A treatment can have remained available and theoretically useful without being more likely than not to have prevented the injury. It might have offered only a modest chance. It might have reduced the severity of the harm without preventing it outright. The clinician shouldn't be pushed toward a certainty the evidence can't support, and the attorney shouldn't be left holding language too vague to actually build a case around. Clinical Intelligence isn't a matter of picking better words — it's explaining, plainly, what the possibility actually amounts to.

A statement about probability only becomes useful once you know exactly what question it's answering. Would earlier treatment probably have prevented the whole injury? Reduced its severity? Delayed progression? Prolonged survival? Preserved some function? Improved the odds of recovery? Those are all different causal claims wearing the same word. A clinician might genuinely believe earlier intervention would probably have improved the outcome without believing the patient would have returned all the way to their prior baseline — the evidence might support reduced disability rather than full prevention. That distinction matters because damages should track the actual causal role the disputed care played. If the care aggravated something that already existed, the case shouldn't be framed as though the care created the whole condition from scratch. If a delay made an injury worse, the harm attributable to that worsening has to be separated out from whatever harm would probably have happened regardless. Probability was never a single, portable conclusion. It has to be pinned to one particular outcome and one realistic alternative.

"Recognized complication" is another phrase that causes its own kind of confusion. A complication can be well known to occur even in the setting of entirely appropriate care — which doesn't mean every single occurrence was unavoidable. Medicine recognizing that something can happen only tells you it can happen. It doesn't answer whether it happened here because of reasonable care or something short of it. There are usually two separate questions hiding inside that one label: was the complication itself avoidable, and once it happened, was it recognized and treated the way it should have been? A bowel injury during surgery might be a well-recognized complication, and the surgical technique might still deserve scrutiny. Even where the injury happened despite entirely reasonable technique, the postoperative response can become its own separate issue if the patient later showed signs of deterioration nobody acted on. A medication reaction can be recognized and unavoidable, while the failure to catch it and stop the medication is not. The label shouldn't be allowed to shut the door on the analysis before the patient-specific questions ever get asked.

Pre-existing risk gets translated too broadly just as often. A patient at high risk of stroke, infection, bleeding, falls, or some other complication — that risk can be clinically important, and it can shape what care was reasonable. It doesn't, on its own, mean the eventual outcome was inevitable. Sometimes high risk actually raises the bar for monitoring or early intervention — the very same factor that explains the injury can also be the reason there was a heightened obligation to watch for it. A patient with vascular disease might be more likely to have a stroke; that doesn't answer whether new neurological symptoms called for further assessment. A patient with chronic kidney disease might be more vulnerable to deterioration, and that vulnerability can make an abnormal result more significant, not less. Risk explains susceptibility. On its own, it never answers responsibility, and it never answers causation.

Attorneys run into records loaded with chronic disease all the time — diabetes, degenerative changes, vascular disease, chronic pain, cognitive decline, reduced mobility, all present before the event even started. Those conditions matter, and they shouldn't be treated as a stand-in for actually understanding the patient's real baseline. Someone can carry several chronic diagnoses and still live independently, drive, work, run a household, take care of family — being medically complex doesn't mean there was no meaningful loss after the event in question. At the same time, whatever happened afterward can't be pinned entirely on the disputed care if part of that decline was already underway, or already likely. So the translation has to stay precise: what could this person actually do before the event? What changed afterward? How much of that change would probably have happened anyway? Pre-existing disease can reduce someone's physiological reserve and make an event's consequences worse. It can also limit how much recovery was ever realistically on the table. The patient's vulnerability doesn't erase the injury. It helps define exactly what the injury actually was.

The word delay tends to sound like it answers more than it actually does. A delay can be obvious — a test ordered late, a result not passed along promptly, treatment that didn't start when it should have — and none of that automatically establishes that the delay caused the injury. What the analysis actually needs is the point where a different response should reasonably have happened, and whether meaningful treatment genuinely remained available at that point. A long interval might contain only a short window where a different response could have changed anything. The earliest symptom isn't always the start of the legally relevant delay — the condition might not have been recognizable yet, the patient might not have been eligible for treatment, the window might have already closed before the disputed failure even occurred. It cuts the other way too — a relatively short delay can be enormously significant when the treatment in question is genuinely time-sensitive. Delay describes time passing. Causation explains what that time actually changed. Treating the two as interchangeable is one of the more common ways a case gets overstated.

Medicine talks about outcomes as multifactorial more often than not — several conditions, decisions, and events all feeding into the final result — and the word contribution can carry wildly different weights depending on the case. A factor can have played a minor role. It can have materially worsened the outcome. It can have sped up something already happening, or created an entirely separate injury. It can be one of several causes without being sufficient on its own to produce the harm. The attorney needs the clinician to spell out the degree and the nature of that contribution: did the disputed care create the harm, aggravate it, accelerate it, prolong it, make it more severe? Would the same outcome probably have happened at roughly the same time regardless of the disputed conduct? Answering those keeps the causal language tethered to the actual patient instead of collapsing into one broad, unqualified conclusion. Contributed is not a word that resolves anything by itself.

Preventable is another one that tends to expand as it moves into legal analysis. An outcome can be preventable in some general medical sense without being preventable for this particular patient, at this particular time, under these particular circumstances. The alternative course has to be realistic: what should have happened instead? Who actually had the authority to make that happen? Was the patient even eligible? Was the necessary treatment actually available? Would the patient likely have accepted it and completed it? A patient might have had a theoretically treatable condition while the treatment itself carried real risk, or the patient was too unstable, presented too late, or had contraindications that closed off the options that otherwise existed on paper. A credible preventability opinion has to account for all of that — describing what probably could have been prevented, and being honest about what probably would have remained regardless.

Unavoidable creates the opposite version of the same problem. A clinician might use it to mean the underlying condition itself couldn't have been prevented. An attorney might hear it as meaning that none of the resulting harm could have been reduced at all. Those are two different conclusions sharing one word. A stroke might not have been fully preventable, and earlier treatment might still have reduced its severity. A surgical complication might have occurred despite entirely reasonable care, while earlier recognition of it might have prevented sepsis or organ damage from following. A patient's death might not have been avoidable in the long run, while negligent care still shortened their survival or caused additional suffering along the way. Whenever an expert calls an outcome unavoidable, it's worth asking which part they actually mean — complete prevention, reduced severity, preserved function, an avoided complication, prolonged survival are all separate questions, and the answer should say plainly where the actual limit of that opinion sits.

Clinicians are trained to communicate uncertainty on purpose, and the phrases they reach for aren't interchangeable even though they can sound similar: consistent with, concerning for, cannot exclude, suggestive of, likely, probable. "Cannot exclude" might mean a condition simply hasn't been ruled out of the range of possibilities. "Consistent with" might mean a finding fits a diagnosis without proving it. "Concerning for" might just flag a level of risk that needs a closer look. What any of them actually means depends on context, on who's using the phrase, and on how much information they had at the time. A radiologist might hedge because the image itself doesn't allow a firm conclusion. A treating clinician might use similar hedging language to justify ordering more tests. An expert looking at the whole record later, with more evidence in hand, might land on something far more definite. None of these should get flattened into one uniform level of certainty just because they sound alike on the page.

The first real shift in meaning tends to happen the moment a detailed clinical record gets summarized. A note describing several competing diagnoses and a plan to reassess can get reduced, in someone's summary, to "the diagnosis was missed." A clinician saying further testing would have been reasonable can turn into a summary claiming the testing was required. An expert who identifies a possible departure but wants to hold off on a final opinion until the original imaging is reviewed can end up described, in some later internal memo, as already supporting a finding of negligence. None of these shifts look dramatic in isolation. Each one, though, pushes the conclusion further than the underlying evidence ever actually went. A genuinely useful summary simplifies the information without changing its level of certainty, its professional source, or its stated limits. If an opinion is preliminary, the summary needs to say so. If it belongs to one specialty, it shouldn't get applied outside that field. If a clinician raised a question rather than answering it, the summary shouldn't quietly turn that question into an answer.

Expert referrals are another spot where the translation can go wrong. An expert should be handed a question shaped by the patient's actual journey and the evidence, not a theory that's already assumed its own answer. A referral asking whether a physician negligently failed to diagnose a stroke starts out with both a legal and a clinical conclusion baked in. A better referral asks whether the patient's symptoms and functional findings required further neurological assessment before discharge — leaving room for the expert to actually examine the real decision point instead of just confirming a foregone conclusion. Causation works the same way: asking flatly whether the delay caused the injury can be too broad a question. The expert may need to weigh whether earlier recognition would probably have prevented the outcome, reduced its severity, or made no real difference at all. How a question gets framed shapes what kind of answer even becomes possible, which is exactly why the goal is to make sure the expert is answering the case the evidence actually presents, rather than the case the original allegation already assumed.

Attorneys also have to translate all of this for clients, which is its own kind of difficult, especially when the client has lived through a devastating outcome and wants a clear answer. Counsel is often trying to communicate real uncertainty without sounding dismissive or evasive. A client can hear "the complication was recognized" and conclude nothing could have been done. They can hear "earlier treatment could have helped" and walk away believing the outcome would certainly have been prevented. What the attorney needs is language that's both accurate and something a person outside medicine can actually hold onto — explaining, for instance, that the care looks concerning but causation is still unresolved, that part of the injury may have been avoidable even though the underlying condition wasn't, that more expert review is needed before anyone can responsibly say how strong the case is. That kind of explanation isn't weakness. It's honest communication with the person who has the most at stake.

Once a matter is actually moving, the language naturally sharpens — a demand, a complaint, a mediation statement, a defense position all need a coherent argument behind them. The risk is that advocacy quietly makes the clinical evidence sound more certain than it is: a cautious opinion becomes definitive, a possible benefit becomes probable prevention, a documentation gap becomes proof that an assessment simply never happened. The same risk runs the other way on defense — a normal result gets presented as though it ruled out every serious condition, a recognized complication gets described as though it were inevitable, pre-existing disease gets stretched to cover losses that were actually new. The whole point of staying disciplined here is to interrupt that drift in either direction. Advocacy was never supposed to require distortion. The strongest position in any case is usually the one that can be traced straight back to the evidence and still hold up under real challenge — which means the language used in negotiation and litigation has to stay faithful to the clinical meaning it grew out of.

It's worth separating translation from interpretation, because they aren't the same thing even though people use them interchangeably. Translation explains what the clinical evidence means in language another professional can actually work with. Interpretation is a professional judgment about the significance of that evidence. A clinician translates a lab trend by explaining why it signals deterioration; the attorney then interprets the legal significance of however the team responded to that deterioration. A qualified expert interprets whether the care fell below the applicable standard; counsel figures out how that opinion fits the governing law and the strategy of the case. Keeping those two functions separate is what protects everyone's professional boundaries — the clinician doesn't get to declare that the defendant was legally negligent, and the attorney doesn't get to independently decide that a clinical finding proves breach or medical causation. The bridge between the two professions only works if everyone stays clear on who's actually responsible for crossing each part of it.

Here's a case built almost entirely around one word. A sixty-four-year-old is admitted after a fall and a head injury. The initial imaging shows no acute bleeding, and the patient stays in the hospital overnight for observation. All through the night, the chart repeatedly describes the patient as stable. Then, hours later, the patient becomes difficult to arouse, and a repeat scan reveals an intracranial hemorrhage.

The family believes the patient deteriorated for hours without anyone responding appropriately. The defense points to the record's repeated use of "stable." Neither position is settled by the word alone. The nursing record shows vital signs staying within an acceptable range the whole night — and it also documents increasing confusion and declining participation in the assessments. One note calls the patient "sleepy but stable." Pain medication had also been given.

Which means the real questions get narrower and more specific. Did "stable" refer only to the vital signs? Was the change in mental status simply expected after the medication, or was it actual neurological deterioration? Were the right neurological checks actually completed? At what point did the change become serious enough to warrant repeat imaging? And, kept deliberately separate from all of that: would earlier imaging probably have changed the treatment, or the outcome?

One honest reading of the evidence shows a progressive change in alertness that was never adequately reassessed and was concerning enough to have justified imaging sooner — and that earlier detection would probably have allowed intervention before the hemorrhage grew as severe as it did. Another honest reading shows early drowsiness consistent with the medication, otherwise reassuring neurological findings, and a hemorrhage that developed quickly after the last reasonable check anyone could have performed. None of that gets resolved by tallying up how many times the chart says "stable." The word's actual meaning has to be reconstructed from the patient's condition, the assessments that were done, the medication given, the timing of the change, and whatever treatment opportunity actually remained. That's the difference between reading a word on a page and understanding what the evidence is actually telling you.

None of this requires law and medicine to start using identical language — each profession keeps its own responsibilities, its own standards, its own way of expressing judgment. What matters is that the meaning survives the trip between them. A cautious clinical observation shouldn't turn into a firm legal conclusion without something more behind it. A complicated medical opinion shouldn't stay so vague that counsel can't actually use it. A preliminary concern shouldn't get presented as final, and a genuine limitation shouldn't quietly vanish just because it complicates the theory of the case. The same discipline runs in the other direction, too — the law's need for a defined position doesn't give anyone license to push the medicine into a certainty it never had. A shared language lets the clinician explain the medicine plainly while holding onto its uncertainty, its scope, its professional limits. It lets the attorney understand what can honestly be concluded, and what still needs another opinion before anyone relies on it. The words in a medical record can look perfectly familiar. That's exactly why it's worth checking whether everyone reading them actually means the same thing by them. The point of translation was never to make clinical language sound more legal. It's to make sure the medical meaning survives the trip into law intact.

Chapter Five: The Limits of Medical Record Review

Medical record review sits underneath almost every case involving injury, illness, or healthcare. Before an attorney can make a responsible decision about anything, somebody has to actually gather the records, work out which encounters matter, locate the diagnoses and treatment, follow the sequence of events, and notice what seems to be missing. That work genuinely matters, and in plenty of cases it gives the attorney exactly what they need.

The trouble starts when a record review gets treated as though it accomplishes more than it was ever designed to. A reviewer can correctly identify every appointment, procedure, test result, medication, consult, and documented change in condition. The events can be arranged into a careful chronology. The final report can be a thorough, faithful summary of everything sitting in the chart — and the attorney can still close the document without actually understanding the case.

Knowing what got documented isn't the same as understanding what was happening to the patient. A summary can tell you the blood pressure fell, the oxygen requirement climbed, urine output dropped, and the patient eventually landed in intensive care. It won't necessarily tell you whether those changes formed a recognizable pattern before the transfer, whether the response stayed reasonable as that pattern developed, or whether escalating care sooner would probably have reduced the severity of the injury. Answering those questions takes more than restating the record. It takes interpreting the evidence against the patient's actual condition, the developing clinical picture, the responsibilities each professional carried, and whatever treatment opportunities were genuinely still on the table.

None of this is a knock on traditional record review or the people who do it well. A lot of reviewers bring real knowledge and produce work that's accurate and genuinely useful. The limitation lives in what the assignment was ever meant to accomplish. Asked to summarize a chart, someone can do that extremely well — the trouble only shows up later, when that summary gets leaned on as though it already answered clinical, causal, or legal questions it was never built to answer.

A summary can be both comprehensive and accurate and still leave the actual issue unresolved. It can walk through years of healthcare, every diagnosis on the problem list, every significant procedure, the whole sequence surrounding the event in question — and the attorney can come away knowing far more about the patient's history while still having no idea where the real clinical concern actually begins. Was the initial care reasonable? When did the level of risk shift? Which professional, or which part of the system, held responsibility at that moment? Did a real treatment opportunity still exist? Did the alleged failure probably change what happened? A good summary hands you the facts needed to explore all of that. Facts don't organize themselves around the decision an attorney actually has to make.

This shows up especially clearly in cases involving deterioration. The record might show several abnormalities developing over time, and a chronology might place them in the right order and show when different professionals got involved. The genuinely important clinical question is whether those abnormalities added up to a recognizable pattern, and whether the care stayed responsive as that pattern developed. The causal question, separately, is whether a different response at that point would probably have led somewhere different. A summary doesn't answer either question just by listing what happened. It gives you the raw material the analysis has to start from.

A large production tends to breed a false sense of reassurance all on its own — when several thousand pages have already been produced, it's tempting to assume nothing important could still be missing. In practice, the size of a production tells you very little about how complete it actually is. Hundreds of those pages might be duplicated reports, repeated histories, billing documents, templated instructions, copied medication lists, routine entries that add almost nothing to the actual issue — while the same production is still missing the original diagnostic images, the medication-administration data, an audit trail, a lab-routing record, a phone log, a transfer-center file, or an outside encounter that would change the whole meaning of the case. The more material there is sitting in front of you, the easier it becomes to assume every important fact must be buried in there somewhere, which is exactly the assumption that stops anyone from asking whether the right evidence was ever actually obtained. A thick production can just be a lot of copies of the same incomplete story. That's why completeness always has to be measured against the actual question being asked — a preliminary screening might work fine with a limited set of records, while a final opinion on delayed recognition, causation, institutional responsibility, or damages needs sources nobody thought to pull during the first pass. The real question was never whether the medical records got produced. It's whether the evidence needed for this specific decision got produced.

Medical records aren't organized around whatever ends up mattering in litigation later. A routine encounter can run several pages once you count the standard templates, medication reconciliation, billing information, and patient instructions padding it out. A critical conversation can live in a single sentence. A sudden functional decline can get recorded briefly in a nursing note and never make it into the physician's summary at all. The length of an entry, and how visible it is, tells you nothing about how important it actually is. A reviewer who follows the volume of the chart can spend a great deal of time on material that barely matters to the case while sailing right past the short entry that changes the entire clinical picture. Clinical importance doesn't always announce itself — sometimes it only becomes visible once a small finding gets connected to some other part of the patient's journey. A brief note that the patient couldn't stand without help can matter more than several pages of chronic diagnoses. A single phone message can mark the exact point where the patient's condition changed. One line in a medication-administration record can reveal that the treatment everyone assumed was given never actually reached the patient. The chart gives every entry a place on the page. It doesn't give every entry its proper weight — that judgment takes actual clinical understanding.

Chronologies are genuinely useful. Medical records are hard to navigate, and a well-built chronology lets an attorney see what happened, and in what order, without wading through the whole chart every time. The danger is mistaking order for meaning. Once every event is sitting on a clean timeline, the case can start to feel more understood than it really is. A chronology might show the patient called the office at nine in the morning, was told to keep taking their medication, called again at two that afternoon, and reached the emergency department at six. The sequence is crystal clear. The questions that actually matter are still wide open: what symptoms were reported on that first call? Were they consistent with the expected course at that point? What changed before the second call? Who took that information, and did they have the authority to act on it? Was the advice reasonable? What treatment remained available during that interval, and how much additional harm probably occurred before the patient finally reached the hospital? A chronology gives you the frame. It doesn't automatically hand you the clinical picture inside that frame. A timeline earns its keep only when it does more than show time passing — when it actually marks where the patient's condition changed, where responsibility shifted from one person or system to another, and when a different response became reasonably necessary. Without that layer of analysis, a chronology can be detailed, entirely accurate, and still useless for guiding an actual legal decision.

Medical records can be read too literally, even when nothing in them is actually wrong. A note says the patient was stable, and the summary just repeats that description without asking whether escalating treatment was the only reason "stable" was even possible. The record says symptoms improved, and the reviewer describes the patient as recovering, when really only one symptom eased, and only for a while. A scan gets called normal, and the summary treats that as ruling out disease altogether, without weighing the timing, the quality of the study, the modality, or its known blind spots. A diagnosis shows up in a later note, and the reviewer unintentionally reads that diagnosis back into the earlier course, as if it had already been known at the time. The words can be copied with total accuracy while the meaning underneath them quietly disappears. Literal accuracy just isn't enough when clinical language depends this heavily on context — the reviewer has to understand what a given statement actually meant for this patient, at this moment. A normal result doesn't answer every clinical question. Less pain doesn't mean a neurological problem resolved. Stable blood pressure doesn't mean a stable mental status. A record review that just repeats the chart's own language, without interpreting what that language actually meant, can hand an attorney false confidence in an understanding the evidence never really supported.

Traditional reviews tend to organize the patient around their diagnoses — diabetes, arthritis, coronary disease, chronic kidney disease, spinal degeneration, chronic pain, a history of falls. Those conditions are relevant, and they can shape risk, prognosis, treatment options, and causation. They don't tell you how the patient was actually living. A diagnosis can look severe on paper while barely limiting the patient day to day. Another condition can look comparatively minor while significantly restricting mobility, cognition, independence, or the ability to work. Without understanding function, a review can end up either exaggerating or minimizing the losses tied to whatever happened. Could this patient walk on their own before the injury? Were they working, driving, managing their own medications, caring for family, living alone? Did they already need help with things? Were their symptoms controlled, and was the underlying condition stable, improving, or already sliding? Those are the questions that actually reveal the baseline — a diagnosis list describes disease, but baseline describes the person. That distinction matters because pre-existing disease gets stretched too far all the time. A medically complex patient can still have suffered a genuinely profound new loss. Another patient might have been heading toward the same decline regardless of whatever's being disputed in the case. The review has to move past the problem list if the attorney is ever going to understand what actually changed.

Record reviews often get requested after a theory has already started to form — the case gets described upfront as a missed diagnosis, a surgical error, a medication injury, a failure to monitor. That framing gives the reviewer somewhere useful to start, and it can also shape the whole review more than it should. Frame the assignment as a missed diagnosis, and the reviewer may spend all their time searching every earlier visit for a chance the condition should have been caught, when the stronger issue might actually be later, when the patient came back worse and simply wasn't reassessed properly. Frame it as surgical negligence, and the reviewer may fixate on the operation itself, when the surgery was performed perfectly reasonably and it's the postoperative response that turned unsafe. A medication case might start out focused on the prescription, when the real issue is in how it was administered, monitored, how it interacted with something else, or how the team responded once signs of toxicity appeared. The allegation is a fine place to start asking questions. It should never be the thing controlling the answer. The patient's actual journey has to be allowed to move the theory, or the whole review risks becoming an expensive exercise in confirming whatever was assumed on day one.

Complex medical records are loaded with abnormal findings — chronic lab abnormalities, longstanding imaging findings, unrelated symptoms, diagnoses with little or nothing to do with the event in dispute. A reviewer can correctly flag every single one of those abnormalities and still leave the attorney with no way to tell which ones actually matter. Which finding changed the level of risk? Which trend should have prompted someone to reconsider the existing plan? Which abnormality connects to the claimed injury, which one supports some competing explanation, and which one genuinely needs a specialist to weigh in? Skip that sorting, and a review can make a case look more alarming purely by racking up the number of abnormal findings described in it. A long list of abnormalities isn't the same thing as a supportable theory. Some findings are just context. Others define the baseline. Only a handful usually control recognition, response, causation, or damages — and the reviewer's actual job isn't to flag everything that's abnormal. It's to explain what's material, and why.

A chart very often shows one event following another: a medication started, symptoms appeared; a procedure performed, a complication followed; treatment given, the patient got worse; a delay occurred, the outcome deteriorated. That sequence can raise a genuinely important causal question. It doesn't answer it. The injury might trace back to the underlying condition, a recognized complication, a different treatment altogether, the patient's own vulnerability, natural progression, or some combination of several of those acting together. Causation needs more than two things happening close in time — it needs an understanding of the biological mechanism, the clinical timing, the treatment opportunity, the patient's eligibility for it, competing causes, and what difference a different course would probably have made. A traditional record review can nail down the sequence precisely without ever testing any of those relationships. This is one of the easiest ways an otherwise accurate report can mislead someone — a chronology can make a connection look obvious purely because two events happened near each other in time, when the real clinical relationship is uncertain, indirect, or simply unsupported. An injury following care doesn't establish that the care caused it. Deterioration following a delay doesn't establish that acting sooner would have changed anything. Those conclusions need real analysis, and very often a qualified expert's opinion behind them.

A record review can accurately identify that a policy wasn't followed, an assessment was incomplete, a message got delayed, or some institutional safeguard failed — and those findings matter, and can point to a genuine professional or systems problem. What the attorney still needs to know is whether that gap actually affected the patient. A result might have been communicated late, after the treatment window had already closed. A medication might have been given incorrectly and then caught and corrected before it caused any harm. A consult might have been delayed without changing the treatment plan at all. A policy might have been breached with no clinical consequence whatsoever. None of that makes the failure irrelevant — it just means the failure and its actual effect need to be examined as two separate things. Standard of care and causation are related, but they aren't the same question, and a record review can identify a possible departure while leaving entirely open how that departure connects to what actually happened to the patient. Keeping those two apart protects the case from two opposite mistakes: treating a real process failure as automatic proof of causation, and letting the absence of complete prevention obscure a genuine worsening of the injury that did happen.

Charts present care through individual names — one person wrote the note, another signed the order, a third appears next to the result. The actual process behind any given entry can be far messier than that. A result can land in a shared queue without ever being assigned to a specific person. A message can get routed to the wrong department. A medication order can simply fail to reach whoever's supposed to administer it. A transfer can stall because there was never an effective escalation pathway to begin with. The person whose name happens to appear in the record can look responsible purely because their part of the process was the visible part. Traditional review can zero in too quickly on whoever documented the event instead of following the actual pathway that information, decision, or responsibility was supposed to travel along. Understanding the case means tracing that process end to end — who noticed the change, who received the information, who had the authority to act, who was supposed to make sure the action actually happened, what system was meant to support all of that, and where exactly it broke down. Sometimes that traces back to one person's failure. Sometimes it reveals institutional responsibility, shared responsibility, or a failure baked into how the system was designed rather than anything one individual did wrong. The chart hands you names. The analysis has to work out actual roles.

The limits of record review cut both ways — they can hide a genuine concern just as easily as they can manufacture unfair criticism. A delay can look unjustified right up until the transfer records show there was no receiving bed available anywhere. A note can look incomplete until another part of the chart shows the assessment did happen. A medication can look like it was skipped until the administration record confirms it was given. An abnormal result can look alarming until you compare it against the patient's own established baseline. A decision can look inexplicable until you understand the competing risks and the actual alternatives that existed. A credible reviewer has to be equally capable of spotting real concern and spotting a reasonable explanation — the goal was never to surface the largest possible number of weaknesses. It's to work out what the full evidence can honestly support. That matters especially when the underlying allegation is emotionally compelling, because a devastating outcome creates real pressure to find an equally serious failure to explain it, when the evidence might instead show reasonable care that simply couldn't prevent an unavoidable result. The reverse happens too — what looks at first like an accepted, garden-variety complication can be hiding a preventable failure to recognize or respond to it. The method has to stay genuinely open to either answer.

A review can cover absolutely everything in the record and still fail to address the one question that actually matters. This tends to happen when the assignment is too broad to begin with — the reviewer summarizes several years of history, dozens of encounters, every medication change, every major diagnosis, and the actual decision point that the whole case turns on gets a few sentences buried somewhere in the middle. The final report ends up comprehensive in volume without being comprehensive in purpose. A genuinely useful review stays tied to the decision the attorney is actually trying to make. Is the immediate question whether the firm should take the case at all? Is counsel deciding whether specialist review is even justified? Does counsel need to know whether the timing supports causation, whether there's institutional exposure, or whether the claimed damages reflect a genuinely new loss? Each of those calls for a different depth and a different focus of review. Without a clear sense of purpose, the work can turn into an expensive restatement of the chart — the attorney ends up with a great deal of information and not much of the understanding needed to actually act on it.

Clinical experience is genuinely invaluable — an experienced clinician can spot a concerning pattern that would sail right past a nonclinical reader. Experience alone, though, doesn't guarantee the evidence gets organized in a way that actually supports a legal decision. A clinician can feel strongly that the care was wrong without ever separating out the clinical concern from professional obligation, systems responsibility, causation, and damages. Another reviewer can produce a beautiful chronology while missing the exact treatment opportunity that controls the causal question. One clinician can describe the medicine accurately while drifting into legal language well outside their lane. Another can stay so cautious throughout that counsel never learns which interpretation the evidence actually favors. A method doesn't replace clinical experience. It helps make that experience visible, consistent, and usable — requiring the reviewer to show how they got to their conclusion, what supports it, what limits it, which questions belong to somebody else's expertise, and what's still genuinely unresolved. That's what makes the analysis easier for an attorney to follow, and easier for a qualified expert to actually test.

Sometimes the limitation starts with what the attorney asks for in the first place. One assignment might ask a reviewer to determine whether negligence occurred, who's responsible, whether causation is established, what damages are recoverable, and what the case is worth — and no single medical review can honestly answer all of that on its own. Some of those questions need legal judgment. Others need formal specialty opinion. Some depend on evidence nobody has obtained yet. Some may stay genuinely uncertain even after a great deal of digging. A responsible review says plainly what it can answer and what it can't. It can identify clinical concerns, reconstruct the patient's journey, separate the reasonable decisions from the questionable ones, and define exactly which issues need expert review — helping counsel understand causation and damages without pretending to any authority over the governing legal standard. Respecting those boundaries doesn't make the review less valuable. It makes it more trustworthy. A report that tries to answer everything can sound wonderfully decisive while quietly resting on conclusions well outside the reviewer's actual expertise or authority.

An early screening review isn't the same thing as a final analysis, and treating them as interchangeable causes real problems. During screening, the attorney mostly needs to know whether the allegation is clinically plausible, which records are missing, what kind of expert this might eventually need, and whether it's worth investing further. That work can proceed with an incomplete evidence base, as long as those limits are stated clearly. A final analysis needs a much sturdier foundation — original imaging, complete baseline records, audit data, testimony, specialist opinions, evidence nobody had access to the first time around. The trouble starts when a preliminary concern quietly gets treated, later on, as a settled conclusion. An early reviewer might reasonably say the care looks concerning and further investigation is warranted; as the case moves forward, that same sentence can get repeated so often it starts sounding like a definitive finding, even though nobody ever actually went and got the additional evidence. What each review was actually meant to be used for should stay visible the whole way through — an opinion that's perfectly fine for preliminary screening may not be remotely fit for a demand letter, an expert referral, a deposition, or a final decision on the case. The level of certainty behind an opinion should always match what it's actually being used for.

Long reports can look more authoritative simply because they're packed with history, medical explanation, and detail — and the attorney's actual question can still go unanswered inside all of it. A review's value was never a function of page count. It comes down to whether the attorney can actually understand what the case is, what supports it, what challenges it, what's missing, what expertise is still needed, and what should happen next. A shorter review that nails those questions can be worth more than a long document that describes everything and lands on no real understanding at all. None of this is an argument for oversimplifying a genuinely complex case — the analysis still needs enough detail to show how the reasoning developed and where the uncertainty actually sits. Detail exists to support understanding. It shouldn't ever become a substitute for it.

None of this means throwing out traditional record review — Clinical Intelligence depends on it. The records still have to be gathered, organized, read, and summarized. Important events still have to be identified, documentation conflicts still have to be located, missing evidence still has to be noticed. The difference is that the work keeps going past mere description. It asks whether the evidence can actually be trusted, who the patient was before any of this happened, what occurred during the critical stretch of time, what the objective findings actually showed, and which professional or system held responsibility at each stage. It asks when the existing plan stopped being enough, what treatment genuinely remained possible, what a different response probably would have changed, and what competing explanation still has to be ruled out. And finally, it connects all of that back to the decision counsel is actually trying to make. This isn't extra information for its own sake — it's the difference between information and understanding. Traditional review organizes the evidence. Clinical Intelligence explains what that evidence actually means for the case.

Not every matter needs the full treatment, either. Traditional record review is valuable on its own and can be entirely sufficient for a straightforward case — it organizes a large production, identifies diagnoses and treatment, builds a chronology, flags abnormal findings, shows where the documentation contradicts itself, and points out what's missing. In plenty of matters, that's genuinely all the attorney needs. The real question was never whether traditional review has value. It's whether the scope of the review actually matches the decision on the table. A simple injury can call for a simple analysis. A complicated case spanning several facilities, uncertain timing, disputed causation, pre-existing disease, and multiple professional roles calls for something more. The depth of the work should scale with the case — nobody needs to manufacture complexity just to prove a framework got used. The attorney should get exactly the level of analysis a responsible decision requires, no more and no less.

Structure, for that matter, can be misused too, and it's worth saying plainly that adding a framework never guarantees a correct result. A well-structured report can still be wrong. The underlying records might be incomplete. The baseline might have been assumed rather than actually established. The timeline might contain incorrect times. Professional roles might have gotten blurred together, and causation might have been overstated. Technology output might have been accepted without anyone verifying it. A reviewer might have worked outside their own expertise, or let the original allegation shape the analysis more than it should have. Headings, diagrams, and a recognized methodology don't create authority just by being present on the page. The actual value lives in the reasoning, the source evidence, how transparent the limitations are, and the professional judgment applied at every stage along the way. The method has to stay open to challenge, correction, revision — its whole job is helping people think more clearly, not giving anyone a shortcut around thinking at all.

Let me give you an example of a case where the chronology pointed everyone toward the wrong event entirely. A fifty-two-year-old has a knee replacement. A few days later they develop shortness of breath and get diagnosed with a pulmonary embolism.

The attorney asks for a medical record review because the patient complained of calf pain before being discharged. The initial review produces a clean chronology: calf pain documented, pain medication given, the patient participated in therapy, discharge the following day, the pulmonary embolism diagnosed two days after that. Read in sequence, it looks like a missed diagnosis.

A closer look changes the actual question. The calf pain was documented after physical therapy and described as muscular — no swelling recorded, no rapid heart rate, no oxygen abnormality, no new decline in mobility at that point. The patient was already on preventive anticoagulation. But after discharge, they called the office reporting sudden shortness of breath. The call itself was documented; how quickly anyone responded, and what advice they actually gave, is a lot less clear.

So the case may never have been about a failure to catch a clot before discharge at all. It may be about the response to that later phone call. A specialist might still conclude the earlier calf pain deserved a closer look — but that can't just be assumed from the chronology on its own.

One honest reading of the evidence shows a recognizable combination of symptoms and risk factors already present before discharge, and that further assessment at that point probably would have led to earlier treatment. It might instead show that the later report of sudden shortness of breath demanded immediate emergency direction, and that whatever delay followed that specific call is what made the injury worse. Another honest reading shows earlier pain entirely consistent with surgery and therapy, preventive treatment already in place, no other warning signs anywhere — an embolism that developed after discharge, met with a response that was actually reasonable given what was known.

The chronology wasn't wrong. It was just incomplete as an explanation. The record review correctly identified what happened. The deeper look identified which of those events actually deserved the real scrutiny — which is really the whole distinction this chapter has been trying to draw.

Before leaning on any record review, it's worth asking what decision the work was actually meant to support, and whether the evidence gathered was enough for that purpose. Was the patient's baseline actually established, or assumed? Was the critical stretch of time interpreted clinically, or just placed in order? Were individual and system responsibility kept separate? Was causation actually examined, or assumed because one thing happened after another? Were the competing explanations addressed? Were the right experts and professional boundaries identified? Does the conclusion actually point toward what should happen next?

A review can be entirely suitable for a preliminary screening and still fall short of a final causal opinion. It might be useful with its limitations clearly stated, or need further clinical analysis, or depend on a specialist's review down the line. There's no weakness in naming those limits honestly. The weakness only shows up when a review gets used for a purpose it was never built to support. Medical record review remains the foundation underneath all of this — it tells you what was documented, what happened, what looks abnormal, what might be missing. Clinical Intelligence doesn't replace that foundation. It asks what all of that information actually means, how the pieces fit together, and what conclusions the evidence can actually carry. The record gives you the material. Understanding is what gives you the case.

A GOVERNING PRINCIPLE

A framework earns trust the same way a diagnosis does:
by holding up, consistently, case after case.

PART TWO

The Method

Chapters Six & Seven

Chapter Six: What Clinical Intelligence Actually Is

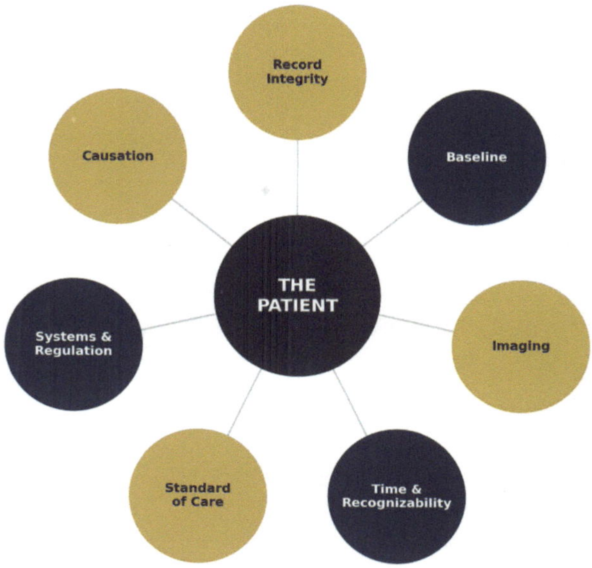

Figure 6.1 — The seven components of Clinical Intelligence, organized around the patient

By now it should be clear that Clinical Intelligence isn't just another name for medical record review, and it isn't a new profession invented to sit somewhere between law and medicine either. It's a structured way of bringing the right questions to the right evidence, in the right order, so that the people responsible for a case can actually understand what the patient experienced and what that experience might mean. That sounds simple enough in one sentence. In practice, it rarely is.

Complex medical cases almost never contain just one problem. There are missing records, uncertain timing, several professionals, multiple facilities, pre-existing disease, contradictory documentation, disputed causation, and a serious outcome that naturally pulls everyone toward a conclusion before the evidence has actually been understood. The attorney is trying to decide whether the matter should even proceed while the clinician is still trying to figure out what was happening to the patient in the first place. An expert can get asked for an opinion before anyone has properly defined the question that opinion is supposed to answer. What this whole approach does is give those separate problems a shared structure — letting the attorney, the clinician, the expert, and everyone else on the case work from the same patient journey, without asking any of them to step outside their own role. The attorney still makes the legal calls. The clinician still interprets the medicine within the honest limits of their training and experience. The qualified expert still owns the specialty opinion. Technology stays a tool that supports the work rather than an authority that decides the case. Clinical Intelligence connects those contributions. It never replaces them.

One of the most common mistakes in a medical case is starting with the allegation. Another is starting with the injury. The better starting point is earlier than both of those — it's the patient. Who was this person before any of this happened? What was their health actually like, and what symptoms already existed? How independently were they living? What treatment were they already on, what risks already existed, and what course was their health likely to take if none of this had ever occurred? Those questions matter because the patient's condition before the event becomes the reference point for everything that follows — without it, whatever changed afterward can get overstated, understated, or just misread entirely. One patient can carry serious chronic disease and still be active, independent, doing fine. Another can have fewer diagnoses on paper and already be sliding significantly. A problem list alone won't tell you which one you're looking at. The first patient might have managed several illnesses successfully for years, kept working, drove regularly, lived without help. The second might have had fewer formal diagnoses while already needing assistance with medication, mobility, daily life. A diagnosis list describes disease. It doesn't necessarily describe the person actually living with it — which is exactly why understanding the patient has to come before anyone starts deciding what was lost, what was caused, or what the case might be worth.

This approach doesn't assume a medical record is complete just because it's long. It asks what's actually been received, what's still missing, what's been copied forward rather than freshly observed, what got entered later than it seems, and what might be sitting in a completely different system. The point isn't to distrust every note or treat the chart as inherently unreliable — it's to understand what each source can actually establish. A physician's note shows the assessment and plan. A nursing record shows how the patient's condition changed and whether the treatment actually worked. A medication-administration record shows whether the ordered drug was actually given. An audit trail can establish exactly when a result became available, or when someone actually opened it. A phone record can confirm contact happened even when the content of that call stays murky. Original imaging can answer a question the written report alone never resolves. None of these sources are competing versions of the case unless they genuinely contradict each other — usually they're just different slices of the same evidentiary picture, and they have to be pulled together before any one of them gets to speak for the whole. That's why treating the evidence carefully isn't preliminary clerical work tucked in before the real analysis starts. It is the reasoning. Every later conclusion about the patient's baseline, the timing of their deterioration, who was responsible, what caused what, and what damages followed all rest on how reliable that underlying evidence actually is.

Chronology matters, but Clinical Intelligence was never meant to just be a more detailed chronology. A list of events tells you what came first and what came after. The patient's journey explains why that sequence actually mattered — asking what was known at each point, how the patient was changing, whether the original plan was working, and when a different response became necessary. It's tracking the changing meaning of the evidence over time, not just the passage of time itself. That's usually where a case actually starts to come into focus. The initial decision may have been perfectly reasonable, and the real problem shows up later, once the patient fails to improve. The first presentation may have genuinely been uncertain, while a second visit contained the warning signs that actually changed the picture. A complication may have been unavoidable while the failure was really in recognizing it, or responding to it while treatment could still have limited the damage. Following the journey lets you find the actual decision point — which isn't necessarily the first symptom, the first visit, or even the moment the condition technically began. It's the point where the available evidence called for a different response than the one it got. Skip that distinction, and a whole stretch of time can get labeled as "delay" even though the condition wasn't yet recognizable, or no real treatment opportunity existed for most of that interval. This approach follows the changing clinical meaning. Not just the clock.

Medical care is almost never delivered by one person acting alone. Information moves through professionals, departments, software systems, and organizational processes that most people never think about until something goes wrong inside one of them. A nurse notices deterioration and passes it to a physician. The physician decides whether more testing, a consult, or a transfer is needed. A lab system releases an abnormal result into a shared electronic queue that then has to assign it to the right person. A pharmacist verifies a medication before it can even be given. A transfer center calls several hospitals before finding an open bed. A monitoring device records a significant change that nobody responsible for responding actually sees right away. Clinical Intelligence follows the care through every one of those steps — asking who knew, who reasonably should have known, who had the authority to act, and where exactly the process broke down. It also asks what system was supposed to support that responsibility, and whether it actually did. This matters because whoever's name appears in the chart isn't necessarily the person who controlled what happened next — the visible name might just belong to whoever documented the event, while the actual responsibility to respond sat somewhere else entirely. A record can make a systems problem look like one person's failure. It can just as easily bury an individual failure inside a complicated system where nobody seems clearly at fault. A fair analysis has to separate those roles out — identifying what each professional actually observed, what information reached them, what authority they held, and what they could reasonably have done, and then looking at whether the systems around them supported that responsibility or got in its way. You can't really understand a patient's care without looking at the people and the processes together.

One of the most important things this approach does is keep professional responsibility and causation as two separate questions. A professional can have acted unreasonably without that automatically meaning the patient's outcome would have been any different. A treatment can have caused an injury without that treatment having been prescribed or performed negligently. A result can have been communicated late, and the treatment window may already have closed before that delay even mattered. So there are really two distinct questions worth asking here: what should reasonably have happened given the circumstances, and what difference would that response probably have made? The first is about professional conduct. The second is about causation. A case can be strong on one and weak on the other — the evidence might show a clear failure to reassess, communicate, or escalate, and still support that the outcome probably wouldn't have changed anyway. Another case might involve a relatively small departure that mattered enormously, because the patient happened to be sitting inside a narrow treatment window at exactly that moment. Both questions need their own independent examination before anyone tries to connect them. That separation is what keeps the analysis from assuming causation just because the care looked poor, and it's also what keeps a real worsening of the injury from getting overlooked just because the whole outcome couldn't have been prevented anyway.

In delayed-care cases, the more useful question is usually not how long the delay lasted, but what actually remained possible during that stretch of time. A long delay can carry almost no causal weight if the injury was already irreversible by the time anyone could have acted. A much shorter delay can matter enormously if the treatment in question was time-sensitive and the patient was still eligible for it. So Clinical Intelligence goes looking for the treatment opportunity itself: when did the condition become reasonably recognizable? What response should have followed at that point? Could the patient actually have received the treatment being discussed? What benefit remained on the table, and what changed during the disputed interval? Answering those sharpens the causal conclusion considerably. Sometimes the evidence supports that earlier care probably would have prevented the injury outright. Sometimes it supports something narrower — reduced severity, preserved function, aggravation, acceleration, prolonged survival. Sometimes it shows that earlier treatment was technically possible but unlikely to have changed much of anything. The method doesn't reach for whichever answer sounds best. It identifies the answer the evidence can actually carry. That discipline matters because the language of "delay" can sound more damning than the underlying medicine actually supports — a long interval can look terrible on a timeline without ever showing that meaningful treatment was genuinely available throughout it. The treatment opportunity is what ties the timing back to the actual outcome.

Every serious medical case has a competing explanation sitting somewhere inside it. Plenty have several. The patient may have had advanced disease, limited physiological reserve, an underlying condition that was going to progress no matter what care they received. A complication may have occurred even though the treatment itself was entirely reasonable. The patient may have delayed seeking help, refused treatment, or shown up after the most effective window had already closed. Another event may account for part of the injury, or several factors may have combined to produce the final outcome together. This approach doesn't just dump those facts into a "limitations" section at the end and carry on as though the preferred theory survives untouched. It asks, honestly, whether the competing explanation actually accounts for the outcome more convincingly. Sometimes it does. Sometimes it only explains part of the harm — limiting the case for complete prevention while still supporting that the disputed care made things measurably worse. Sometimes it explains why a patient was especially vulnerable while also revealing why the level of monitoring should have been higher, not lower. A competing explanation can weaken one part of a case while strengthening another part entirely. Pre-existing disease can reduce the odds of a full recovery and also make a worsening trend more significant, not less. A recognized complication can explain why something happened while doing nothing to explain why nobody caught it or treated it sooner. A fair method has to let all of those distinctions stay visible instead of collapsing them into one tidy verdict.

The real value of Clinical Intelligence was never that it spits out one final answer automatically. Its value is in sharpening the questions before anyone goes looking for an answer at all. A broad request asking an expert simply "did malpractice occur" crams too many separate issues into one question — professional responsibility, causation, and legal significance, all before anyone's even identified the actual clinical decision point. A much more useful set of questions asks when the patient's condition became reasonably recognizable, what response that called for, whether the patient remained eligible for the treatment being proposed, and what probably would have changed had that treatment started then. The expert may also need to sort out what part of the injury was already there to begin with, and what competing cause has to be ruled out. Questions like that are simply more precise, and they let the expert answer from within their actual specialty and role, rather than being asked to render a verdict on the whole case. They also help counsel figure out which expert is actually needed in the first place — a case turning on imaging needs a radiologist's read, a case turning on surgical technique needs a surgeon in that specific field, a question about nursing monitoring or escalation calls for different expertise than a question about a physician's diagnostic judgment. This approach doesn't answer any of those specialty questions itself. It helps counsel aim the right question at the right professional.

A structured method can make a medical case a lot easier to follow. That doesn't make everyone involved qualified to render every opinion. A clinical reviewer might identify that the original imaging is central to the whole case — a qualified radiologist still has to actually interpret those images. A nurse might flag a concern involving monitoring, communication, or escalation, while a physician expert is still needed for the formal opinion on a physician's own diagnosis or treatment. An attorney can understand the causal pathway clearly enough to direct discovery, prepare witnesses, and evaluate the case, without that turning counsel into the medical expert. Clinical Intelligence makes professional boundaries easier to see. It should never be used to erase them. It's most credible exactly when every professional's contribution stays inside its proper scope — a clinician explaining what the evidence means medically without drifting into legal conclusions, an expert addressing the specific specialty question rather than rendering a verdict on the whole case. The attorney then takes those contributions and makes the actual legal decision. Connection was never meant to mean replacement.

This approach shouldn't be reserved for cases that already look strong. A lot of its value shows up much earlier than that. At intake, it can show that an alleged event is clinically plausible and worth digging into further. It can flag records that need to be preserved before they're lost or overwritten. It can reveal that the original theory is too broad, that the patient's actual baseline changes the whole damages picture, or that one focused expert opinion is worth getting before anyone spends more money on the case. It can also show that the case shouldn't go forward at all — and that's not a failure of the method. It's one of the most valuable things it can do. A responsible early look can save enormous time, cost, and emotional investment in a theory the evidence simply can't carry. It can also stop a genuinely strong case from getting rejected just because the first version of the allegation was vague, or because the medical record was hard to make sense of on a first pass. The whole point is improving the decision, not guaranteeing that every matter moves forward.

A fair method asks the same questions no matter who's paying for the review. For plaintiff's counsel, Clinical Intelligence might surface a clearer professional failure, an overlooked institutional problem, or a stronger causal pathway than the original theory ever identified. It might just as easily show that the outcome wasn't preventable, or that the claim needs to be narrowed. For defense counsel, it might support that the care was reasonable, that causation is limited, or that most of the loss traces back to the underlying disease rather than anything anyone did wrong. It might also reveal that the existing defense position is overlooking a genuine delay, a communication failure, or an institutional weakness nobody wants to look at too closely. The questions don't change depending on who's asking. The evidence might point somewhere different depending on the case, but the method stays the same — record integrity, baseline, timing, responsibility, treatment opportunity, causation, competing explanations, all examined with the same discipline regardless of which side commissioned the work. That consistency is exactly what gives the final conclusion any credibility at all.

Some settings use structured classifications, matrices, or scoring tools alongside this approach, and those can genuinely help with organizing information, flagging risk, or comparing different parts of a case. They should never be mistaken for the conclusion itself. A case can look strong across several categories on a matrix and still fail because one essential causal question simply can't be supported. Another can be riddled with documentation problems while resting on a weak theory of professional departure. A numerical score can't explain why an abnormal finding actually mattered, when responsibility shifted from one person to another, or what a different response would probably have changed. The reasoning has to stay visible the whole way through — if a case can't be explained without pointing back at the score, the analysis simply isn't finished yet. A tool can support professional judgment. It can never substitute for it.

Technology can support this whole approach a great deal — sorting, searching, comparing, extracting, organizing enormous volumes of information, spotting repeated patterns, locating missing documents, cutting down the time spent on repetitive work. It can also make mistakes very quickly, and present them very convincingly. It might confuse an order with an actual administration of a drug, treat language copied forward as though it were a fresh observation, or infer causation purely from sequence. It might stitch records together incorrectly, miss a patient-identity mismatch, or produce a smooth, coherent-sounding narrative out of evidence that was never actually complete. Which is exactly why this approach has to stay accountable to human judgment at every step. Somebody has to verify the source. Somebody has to actually understand the patient. Somebody has to decide whether a conclusion sits within the reviewer's real professional scope, and somebody has to be the one responsible once the final work gets signed off on. Technology can assist the analysis. It should never be handed authority over it.

Some cases stay genuinely uncertain even after the most careful review anyone can give them. The exact time something started may never be pinned down. A critical conversation may never be fully reconstructed. Qualified experts may reasonably disagree about what the evidence actually means. The probable benefit of some treatment may only ever be knowable as a range rather than a number. A patient's future course may not be cleanly separable from the disease they already had. This approach shouldn't hide any of that uncertainty, or dress it up in polished language until it sounds like certainty. It should name it plainly. From there, the attorney can decide whether that uncertainty can actually be narrowed through more records, more testimony, more expert analysis, more discovery — or whether it simply has to be managed as part of the litigation, or, sometimes, whether it should stop the matter from moving forward responsibly at all. A method isn't weakened by admitting what it can't know. It becomes more trustworthy, precisely because its conclusions reflect the real limits of the evidence rather than papering over them.

Used well, this whole approach helps everyone involved actually see the same case. It can make an enormous medical record manageable without flattening the patient's journey into something simplistic. It can reveal the exact point where a patient's course changed, and identify who held responsibility at that moment. It can separate a genuine failure from an outcome that simply wasn't related, and tell an unavoidable condition apart from preventable harm layered on top of it. It can help an attorney figure out which expert is actually needed and hand that expert a question they can actually answer. It can improve how counsel talks to the client — explaining what the evidence supports, what's still uncertain, and why the theory of the case might need to move. It can show why a case should go forward. It can just as easily show why it shouldn't. Its real strength was never that it always turns up more. It's that it helps everyone actually understand what's already there.

Any structured method can turn rigid if it gets applied mechanically, and that's worth guarding against constantly. Professionals can start filling in sections instead of actually thinking about the patient. The vocabulary can become familiar while the reasoning underneath it stays shallow. A diagram can make a genuinely disputed sequence look settled. A classification can create a sense of certainty the underlying evidence never earned. A reviewer can grow overconfident purely because the finished structure looks comprehensive on the page. That's exactly why this approach has to stay open to challenge — the evidence traceable, the assumptions visible, and any identified limitation actually allowed to affect the final conclusion. Most importantly, the case has to stay capable of changing. The method should never be used to protect an original theory just because a lot of work has already gone into it. The whole framework exists to support judgment. Not to replace it.

Let me walk through an example. A sixty-one-year-old with diabetes and chronic kidney disease is admitted to the hospital with fever, weakness, and confusion. Antibiotics are started, and the patient initially seems to improve. Over the next twelve hours, their blood pressure starts falling, their oxygen needs climb, and urine output drops. They're eventually transferred to intensive care with septic shock.

A traditional review might note, correctly, that antibiotics were given promptly and that the transfer happened once the patient became unstable. Both of those things can be true. The deeper question is whether the patient's condition showed a recognizable failure of the original plan before that transfer ever happened.

The baseline matters here because chronic kidney disease can affect how you read lab values and can reduce someone's ability to tolerate an infection — which doesn't mean the later organ injury was inevitable, or that the changes in urine output didn't matter. The timeline matters because the deterioration didn't happen at one clean, obvious moment — it built up across several separate observations, each of which might have looked minor in isolation. The treatment response matters because the apparent improvement after starting antibiotics may have been temporary; a brief drop in fever or a moment of clearer thinking doesn't establish that the infection was actually under control if everything else was quietly getting worse. The professional roles matter too — nursing staff may have documented every one of these changes while the authority to alter the treatment plan or escalate care sat somewhere else, with the information passing through several hands before anyone actually made a decision. And the system around all of those people deserves its own look: was there a clear pathway for escalating worsening findings? Did the changes get communicated together as one developing pattern, or did each one land with a different person in isolation?

The causation question stays separate from all of that. Earlier escalation might have reduced how severe the organ damage got without preventing septic shock outright. One honest reading of the evidence shows the falling blood pressure, rising oxygen needs, and dropping urine output forming a recognizable pattern that called for intervention sooner — and that the resulting delay made the organ dysfunction worse, or longer-lasting, than it needed to be. Another honest reading shows deterioration that simply happened fast despite appropriate treatment, with a transfer that occurred within a perfectly reasonable window once the picture actually changed.

This approach doesn't decide which of those readings is correct before the evidence has actually been tested. What it does is make sure the case never gets flattened down to "antibiotics were given" or "the patient got critically ill later." It brings the whole journey into view instead.

This approach isn't another person sitting in the room. It's the structure that helps everyone already in that room understand the same patient. It helps the clinician explain what the evidence means medically, including exactly where it's uncertain or needs a specialist's read. It helps the attorney understand what that medical meaning might mean for the legal decision sitting in front of them. It helps the expert receive a focused question instead of a broad theory that's already assumed its own answer. And it helps everyone involved see where the record actually ends, and where professional judgment has to begin. This approach should make a case easier to understand without ever making it look more certain than it actually is. It doesn't replace expertise. It just gives that expertise a place to meet, around one patient's journey.

Chapter Seven: How the Shared Language Emerged

Clinical Intelligence didn't start as an effort to invent anything. There was no diagram on a wall somewhere, no predetermined list of pillars, no decision that medical-legal work needed one more framework added to the pile. It started much more simply, with the repeated, low-grade frustration of watching genuinely intelligent, experienced professionals work through complicated cases without ever quite reaching the clarity all that effort should have produced.

The records were often enormous, and the central issue still stayed stubbornly hard to pin down. The chronologies were detailed, and they didn't always explain when the patient's condition actually changed, or why that change mattered. Attorneys and clinicians were reading the same words and hearing different things. Expert referrals were often broad enough to invite an opinion without ever really defining the question the case actually needed answered. Causation had a habit of showing up near the end of a review as though it simply followed from the sequence of events — there had been a delay, the patient had deteriorated, and the two got connected without anyone fully checking whether useful treatment was even still available, or what part of the outcome a different response would actually have changed.

None of this was because people weren't working hard. They were working extremely hard. The more interesting question was why all that effort could still leave an attorney genuinely unsure what the case actually was. That question led to another. And then another.

Why was a patient's baseline treated as background information, a footnote before the "real" story started, instead of the actual starting point for understanding the injury? Why did record productions get called complete when the original imaging, the communication data, the audit histories, the medication-administration records were nowhere in them? Why was delay so often measured from the first symptom rather than from the point where the available information actually called for a different response? Why did individual professionals keep getting blamed for failures that a system around them had actually created? Why did professional departure and causation keep blurring into each other so easily? Why did the original legal theory sometimes stay frozen in place even after the clinical evidence had clearly moved somewhere else?

The structure that eventually became Clinical Intelligence grew out of following those questions, one at a time. Understanding came first. The design came a long time after.

Most complicated medical cases don't actually suffer from a lack of information. They suffer from information that's never been connected. The chart can hold the patient's history, the observations, the labs, the imaging, the treatment, the consults, the outcome — spread across thousands of pages, several facilities, a handful of incompatible software systems. All of it present. None of it necessarily understood. A chronology can put every single event in the right order and still leave the attorney with no idea which one of those events actually mattered most. A clinician can flag care that looks concerning without ever explaining whether that concern points toward a professional departure or a causal conclusion — two very different things. An expert can produce a medically sound opinion that answers a completely different question from the one the case actually needed answered, focusing on whether a diagnosis was theoretically possible when the real issue was reassessment, or communication, or how the team responded to deterioration. The gap was never really between the record and the person reading it. It was between the different kinds of reasoning being applied to the exact same evidence — medicine trying to understand what happened to the patient, law trying to determine what could be established and what significance should follow from it. Those two ways of thinking needed a place to actually meet.

Before it was even possible to ask what happened, it turned out to be necessary to ask whether the evidence in hand was good enough to answer that question at all. That sounds almost too basic to say out loud, and it kept getting skipped anyway. A production got treated as complete simply because it was large. Duplicate records created the illusion that a single finding had been independently confirmed several times over. Orders got read as proof that treatment actually happened. Written imaging reports got relied on without anyone ever pulling the original studies. Notes entered or signed hours later got treated as though they'd been written in real time. A result showing up somewhere in the electronic system got confused with evidence that the responsible clinician had actually laid eyes on it.

So the first real question, the one everything else had to sit on top of, turned out to be about the integrity of the evidence itself. What records had actually been produced? What was still missing? Did every page genuinely belong to this patient? Were the timestamps being read for what they actually represented? Did a given system entry show when information became available, when it got routed somewhere, or when a person actually opened it? Was repeated language the product of repeated observation, or had it just been copied forward from an earlier note? Could every significant conclusion be traced back to something reliable? Those questions made it obvious that no later analysis could ever be sturdier than the evidence underneath it. Checking that integrity was never administrative housekeeping to clear out of the way before the real work started. It was the foundation the clinical and legal reasoning both had to stand on.

The next question that kept coming up was who the patient had actually been. Medical cases tend to start at the moment of the alleged injury, with everything before that point compressed down into a list of diagnoses, medications, and risk factors. That left the patient's whole earlier life sitting in the background, even though every conclusion about injury, causation, and damages depends on knowing what existed there. A patient with chronic spinal disease might have worked full-time without restriction. A patient with advanced lung disease might have lived independently, managing every part of their own daily life without help. Another patient, with a comparatively short list of diagnoses, might already have needed substantial help because of cognitive impairment, frailty, or a decline that was already well underway. There was no fair way to understand what came later without that comparison sitting alongside it.

Which is where the idea of establishing an honest baseline came from. It was never meant to produce a longer medical history for its own sake. It was meant to produce an accurate picture of the actual person: what could this patient do before the event? What symptoms already existed? What treatment and support were already in place? Was the underlying condition stable, improving, or already declining — and what was likely to happen even if none of the disputed events had ever occurred? That baseline became the first honest point of comparison in the whole method. It kept the case from treating every later problem as brand new, and it kept the patient from being reduced to a diagnosis list that quietly erased however much independence and function they actually had.

Chronology had always been part of medical record review. The problem was that dates and times kept showing up with no clinical meaning attached to them. A sequence could show that several hours passed without showing when a legally and clinically relevant delay actually began. The first symptom, the first visit, the final diagnosis — all visible points on a timeline, and none of them automatically marked the moment where a different response became necessary. The point that actually mattered, more often than not, was when the available information should reasonably have changed the plan.

That called for a different kind of timeline entirely — one asking when the patient's condition actually began to change, and when that change became visible to someone. Who had access to the information, and what did they understand from it? What action followed, and did the patient respond the way anyone expected? At what point did the existing explanation, or the existing plan, simply stop making sense? Reconstructing the timeline this way came out of realizing the case never really turned on time passing by itself. It turned on the changing meaning of the patient's condition during that time. This distinction also stopped delay from getting measured too broadly — a disease can exist before it's recognizable, a symptom can appear before it reasonably demands another intervention. The interval that actually matters starts when the evidence supports a different response, not simply whenever the first symptom can be spotted in hindsight.

Imaging kept getting treated as just another line in the chronology — a report gets quoted, its date gets noted, and the review moves on. That was never enough. Imaging can offer objective evidence of injury, progression, mechanism, and the relationship between something chronic and something acute. It can show what changed and help pin down when that change became visible. It also has real limits — the significance of any study depends on timing, the modality used, technical quality, the clinical information behind it, how it was interpreted, and whether there was anything to compare it against. A later scan can show catastrophic damage without ever establishing when the injury actually became irreversible. An early study can get called normal without ruling out a condition that was still developing, or simply wasn't detectable by that particular modality. The written report doesn't always answer the question the case ends up needing answered — sometimes the original images themselves need a qualified expert's eyes on them. Imaging analysis had to become its own distinct piece of the method, because objective visual evidence just can't be treated the same way as ordinary narrative documentation. It needed its own discipline, its own context, its own professional boundaries.

Clinical reviewers can often sense fairly quickly that something about the care feels wrong, and that instinct is genuinely valuable — it points toward the part of the journey that deserves a closer look. Concern, though, is not yet an opinion about the standard of care. An omitted assessment, a delayed response, an incomplete note, a policy that wasn't followed — none of that can be understood without weighing the professional's actual role, the setting they were working in, the information they had, and what reasonable options genuinely existed at the time. The question had to get more specific than "something feels off": what should this professional, in this role, holding this information, reasonably have done? That became the real basis of any standard-of-care review inside the model. It was never enough to point out that another course of action existed — medicine allows more than one acceptable approach most of the time. The analysis had to explain why some other course was actually required, not merely preferable. It also had to stay genuinely open to the possibility that the original decision was reasonable all along; a bad outcome doesn't automatically turn every alternative into an obligation. The method needed a way to tell apart reasonable care, legitimate professional concern, a possible departure, and the kind of question that genuinely needs a formal expert opinion behind it.

A lot of cases start out looking like they're about one professional's conduct. Look wider, and responsibility is often spread across an entire system instead. An abnormal result lands in a shared queue and never gets assigned to anyone. A nurse escalates a concern and the message never reaches whoever actually has the authority to change the plan. A physician enters a perfectly appropriate order, and the treatment simply never gets carried out. A transfer gets requested, and there's no process for escalating things further when no receiving bed can be found anywhere. Healthcare runs through systems — those systems decide whether information reaches the right person, whether the safeguards actually work, whether a clinical decision ever turns into an action. Looking at the regulatory and institutional layer surrounding a clinician came out of realizing you simply can't fairly judge individual conduct without understanding the structure it was operating inside. The question was never just whether a policy existed, or whether someone technically followed every written step. The more useful question was whether the safeguard actually worked the way it was supposed to, and whether its failure changed anything for the patient. A policy shows how an organization expected information to move. On its own, it doesn't establish negligence or causation — the analysis still has to work out who actually held responsibility, whether the process itself was reasonable, where exactly it broke down, and what difference that breakdown probably made.

Causation kept getting treated as something you could just infer from the order events happened in. Care was delayed, and the patient got worse. A medication was given, and an injury followed. A diagnosis was missed, and the eventual outcome was severe. Those sequences raise real causal questions. They don't answer them. The analysis had to actually dig into the biological mechanism, the treatment opportunity, whether the patient was even eligible for it, the competing causes sitting in the background, and the specific difference a different response probably would have made. That became what this book calls causation mapping — not just asking whether the disputed event caused the injury, but working out what part of the final outcome could fairly be pinned on it. Did the conduct create the injury outright, or make it worse? Did it aggravate something that already existed, speed up a decline, prolong treatment, shorten survival? Would some, or all, of the same outcome probably have happened regardless? The answer usually ended up narrower than the original allegation — and more defensible, too, because it followed the patient's actual course instead of chasing the broadest theory available. Being able to tell complete prevention apart from partial aggravation gives an attorney a much sturdier foundation for strategy, expert selection, and how damages get analyzed.

A medical review could be thoughtful, balanced, and clinically accurate, and the attorney could still close it not knowing what to do next. That exposed the last real gap: analysis has to become something an attorney can actually act on. Counsel needs to know what the evidence supports, what challenges the working theory, and what's still missing. Counsel needs to know which expert is actually required, what to investigate next, and whether the matter should move forward, narrow, pivot, settle, defend, or simply stop. That's where the idea of a genuinely litigation-ready output came from — because understanding has pretty limited practical value if nobody can actually use it responsibly. That never meant converting clinical analysis into legal advice; the attorney still owns the law, the procedure, the strategy, the final call. It meant presenting the medical evidence in a form that let counsel exercise that judgment with a much clearer view of the patient's actual journey — preserving the uncertainty, naming the professional boundaries, telling preliminary findings apart from formal opinions, and showing exactly how the conclusion got reached. It also had to be useful enough to actually point toward the next move.

There was never one single moment when the whole model just appeared, fully formed. It grew gradually. Every recurring problem exposed another question nobody had answered yet, and every new question changed how the earlier pieces had to be understood. Checking the integrity of the evidence changed how the timeline got built, because the times and events couldn't be trusted until their sources had been verified. Establishing the baseline changed how injury and damages got described, because the patient's prior condition supplied the comparison everything else needed. Reconstructing the timeline changed how professional responsibility got examined, by pinpointing exactly where the clinical meaning shifted. Imaging changed the understanding of timing, mechanism, objective injury. Looking at the surrounding system changed how responsibility got assigned. Mapping causation changed how damages got tied back to the conduct actually in dispute. And the need for a genuinely useful final output changed how every earlier piece of the analysis had to be communicated in the first place.

The name Clinical Intelligence came after all of that reasoning, not before it. The work already existed. The name just gave it something to be recognized by, explained by, taught, repeated. That order matters, because this methodology was never designed first and then imposed on later cases. It was recognized through the work itself, one frustrating case at a time.

The word intelligence can sound, out of context, like a claim to superior knowledge, or some kind of authority over the professionals actually doing the work. That isn't what it's meant to say here. Intelligence, in this sense, just means the ability to bring information into a meaningful relationship with itself. A medical record holds data. Clinical Intelligence asks what that data actually means for this patient, at this moment, within this specific care pathway, for the decision that now has to get made. It isn't a claim that one person knows more than everyone else in the room. It's a discipline of connection — connecting the patient to the record, the record to the clinical course, the course to professional and systemic responsibility, that responsibility to the treatment opportunity, and the treatment opportunity to the outcome. Then, carefully, connecting the medical analysis to the legal decision without merging the two into one. The intelligence was never sitting in a job title, a report, a diagram, or a piece of software. It lives in the quality of the reasoning, and in how reliable the connections actually are.

As all of this developed, another benefit became obvious: attorneys and clinicians could start using the same questions without needing to do each other's jobs. The attorney could ask whether the patient's baseline had actually been established without becoming the clinician responsible for interpreting it. The clinician could point to evidence of a likely systems failure without ruling on the institution's legal liability. The expert could focus tightly on the treatment opportunity or the specialty question without having to reconstruct every administrative detail of the case. Other professionals could contribute evidence about systems, operations, technology, or safety without claiming clinical or legal authority they never had. The questions themselves became the meeting point. Checking the evidence's integrity gave everyone the same evidentiary foundation to stand on. The baseline gave them the same picture of the pre-event patient. Reconstructing the timeline gave them the same sequence and the same decision points. Imaging gave them the same objective evidence. Looking at professional roles and systems gave them the same care pathway to examine. Mapping causation gave them the same claimed difference in outcome to argue about. The professionals could still land in different places — agreement was never actually the point. What changed was that they were no longer disagreeing from entirely different versions of the same case.

None of this could become a credible shared language if it only worked for one side. The same structure had to be equally capable of showing that care was unreasonable or that it was entirely reasonable. It had to be able to identify a professional failure without assuming that failure caused harm. It needed to recognize when an outcome truly was unavoidable, when responsibility actually sat with a system rather than one person, and when pre-existing disease genuinely limited what damages could be attributed to the disputed event — while also recognizing that pre-existing disease can just as easily raise the stakes and make careful monitoring more important, not less. It had to be able to conclude that more evidence was needed, or that the matter shouldn't proceed at all. Neutrality here was never about avoiding firm conclusions. It's about letting the evidence decide the direction and the strength of whatever conclusion gets reached. That principle was baked in from the start, because the whole thing grew out of questions, not out of advocacy. The questions were never designed to prove a theory. They were designed to find whatever the earlier kinds of review had been missing.

Every part of this had to keep coming back to the patient. Did the missing record actually matter to the patient's care? Did the baseline change how the injury should be understood? Did the timeline show when the condition became recognizable, or when the original plan stopped working? Did the imaging actually clarify what happened? Did the professional or systemic failure change the care the patient received? Did another response remain capable of helping? What additional harm did this particular patient actually experience? Without that constant return to the patient, the whole method risked becoming just another abstract framework — sounding sophisticated while drifting further and further from the person whose journey it was supposed to be explaining. The patient's journey is what kept it grounded. A question only earned its place if it actually improved the understanding of what happened to this patient, or supported a fairer decision about the case.

A method that grows out of repeated real-world problems has a real strength to it: every part of it exists because something meaningful kept getting missed without it. Checking the evidence's integrity isn't the first step simply because every model needs a beginning somewhere — it's there because incomplete, unreliable evidence kept producing conclusions that didn't hold up. Establishing a baseline isn't there to pad out the review — it's there because injury and damages simply can't be measured without knowing who the patient was before any of this happened. Mapping causation isn't there to make a report sound more sophisticated — it's there because professional departure kept getting mistaken for patient harm, over and over. The structure is practical because the questions grew out of practical failures. Every piece of it has an actual reason to exist, addressing some recurring gap in how complicated medical evidence was being understood and communicated.

A method that grows naturally out of experience can still calcify once it gets written down and formalized, and that's a real risk worth naming honestly. Professionals can start believing every case needs the exact same amount of analysis. It doesn't. A straightforward matter shouldn't get needlessly complicated just to prove every piece of the method got touched. A genuinely difficult case shouldn't get squeezed into an oversimplified shape because a template only has so much room on the page. These ideas are meant to guide thinking. They were never meant to become boxes filled in mechanically. How much any one of them matters will shift from case to case — imaging might control one matter entirely and barely register in another. Looking at systems might be central to a communication failure and largely beside the point in a question about one isolated surgical technique. And the method itself has to keep evolving, because healthcare changes, medical evidence changes, technology changes, professional roles shift over time, and legal standards and evidentiary requirements move too. Clinical Intelligence should hold onto its central discipline without ever pretending its current form is finished. Something that started by refusing to stop asking questions has to stay willing to keep asking them about itself.

Here's an example of what it looks like when the inquiry actually moves away from the first allegation. A fifty-nine-year-old has abdominal surgery. Two days later they're increasingly uncomfortable, their heart rate is climbing, and they're producing less urine. A later scan confirms a postoperative leak.

The initial allegation is surgical negligence. The operative report doesn't describe a recognized injury during the procedure, and a qualified surgical reviewer finds the technique reasonable, explaining that this kind of complication can occur without any negligence at all. At first glance, that opinion looks like it settles the whole case.

Following the patient's actual journey raises a different question entirely. The postoperative record shows a gradual decline — pain medication increased, mobility dropping, heart rate climbing across several separate assessments, urine output falling. Different professionals documented each of those changes, and none of them ever showed up together in one note. Looked at separately, every single finding might have seemed minor. Looked at as one developing pattern, they might have called for an entirely different response.

Checking the evidence's integrity reveals that some of the medication-administration detail and parts of the fluid-balance record are missing. The baseline shows the patient was active and fully independent before the surgery. Reconstructing the timeline shows the deterioration built up over many hours rather than appearing suddenly. The imaging helps pin down when the leak actually became visible, and what an earlier study might reasonably have shown. The standard-of-care question shifts away from the operative technique itself and toward the postoperative reassessment and rescue that should have followed. Looking at the system means examining how the nursing concerns were actually communicated, and who held the authority to escalate the care. And mapping causation asks whether catching this sooner probably would have reduced the severity of the infection, avoided some of the organ injury, shortened the ICU stay, or improved the eventual recovery.

The evidence might show the operation was reasonable and the postoperative response wasn't. It might show both the procedure and the later care fell within an acceptable range. It might support partial causation rather than complete prevention. The case becomes understandable precisely because the inquiry was allowed to move. The initial allegation stayed a starting point. It was never a fixed destination — and that's exactly how this whole method came to exist in the first place.

Clinical Intelligence never started with a diagram. It started with questions that the existing forms of review simply weren't answering. Why was the patient disappearing inside their own medical record? Why were attorneys and clinicians using the same familiar words while understanding them completely differently? Why could a timeline be perfectly accurate and still fail to explain what time actually meant, clinically? Why did a professional failure keep getting treated as causation before anyone tested whether it actually changed the outcome? Why did the wrong people sometimes end up blamed? Why did a theory of the case stay frozen in place once the medical evidence had clearly moved somewhere else?

The method emerged by simply refusing to stop asking those questions. Each one uncovered another piece of the patient's journey that needed understanding, and the accumulated answers slowly revealed a structure underneath them. That structure came later. It was never built to tell attorneys, clinicians, or experts what to think. It was built to help them see what their separate ways of looking at a case might otherwise miss entirely. That's exactly why it works as a shared language. It doesn't ask the professions to become the same thing. It just gives them a reliable way to meet, around the same patient.

A GOVERNING PRINCIPLE

Ask the same question in both languages: what happened to this patient, and when could it have been known?

PART THREE

The Framework in Practice

Chapters Eight Through Fourteen

Chapter Eight: Record Integrity as the Common Foundation

Before anyone can agree on what a medical case actually means, they need to be looking at the same evidence. That sounds obvious enough. In practice, it's often exactly where the first misunderstanding starts.

An attorney might believe the complete medical record has been produced. A clinician might review the hospital chart and never actually receive the original imaging. An expert might get handed a selected set of records and a chronology without ever learning that later documents, phone records, or audit data even exist. Everyone can say, in perfectly good faith, that they've reviewed the case, when in reality each person has reviewed a slightly different version of it. The discussion can get remarkably detailed before anyone notices that the foundation underneath it is incomplete — and by that point, the disagreement tends to get chalked up to professional perspective, or specialty, or interpretation, when the real problem is a lot simpler than that. The professionals just aren't working from the same evidence.

That's why checking the integrity of the record comes first in this whole approach. It was never clerical work to clear out of the way before the meaningful analysis begins. It is part of the analysis. Every later conclusion about the patient's baseline, the critical timeline, professional responsibility, causation, and damages depends on whether the evidence underneath it is complete enough, and reliable enough, for the question actually being asked. A case simply can't become clearer than its own foundation allows.

Medical productions tend to be large, and that size can feel reassuring all on its own — when thousands of pages show up, it's natural to assume every important part of the patient's care must be represented somewhere in there. That assumption isn't always safe. A thousand-page production can hold hundreds of duplicates, repeated medication lists, templated instructions, billing documents, copied histories — all of that volume creating the appearance of completeness while the evidence that actually controls the case is nowhere to be found. What's missing might be the original imaging, a nursing flowsheet, a medication-administration record, a lab-routing log, a patient portal message, a transfer-center record. It might be an outside emergency visit that got mentioned in passing and never actually produced. It might be a prior functional assessment that would explain exactly how independently the patient was living before the event. It might be an electronic audit history showing when a critical result became available, and whether anyone ever actually opened it. The page count tells you how much material arrived. It doesn't tell you whether the right material arrived — which is a large part of why a medical case can stay genuinely unclear despite a huge amount of work going into it. The review gets deeper and more detailed, and the actual evidentiary gap sits there unnoticed the whole time. Part of the job is spotting that gap before a conclusion gets built on top of it.

No record set is complete in some abstract sense. It's complete enough, or not complete enough, for a particular purpose. A preliminary screening review might not need every document ever created during the patient's care — counsel may only need enough to decide whether the allegation is clinically plausible, whether anything urgently needs to be preserved, and whether further investigation is worth the money. A final causation opinion needs a great deal more. A case turning on delayed recognition can depend on precise timing, communication records, the original imaging, whether the patient was even eligible for the treatment in question, and evidence showing what remained possible at each point along the way. A damages analysis can need years of baseline records, functional assessments, rehab documentation, later care, evidence of the patient's actual work and daily responsibilities. A question about institutional responsibility can require staffing records, policies, routing systems, audit trails — operational evidence that never shows up in an ordinary patient chart at all. Which is why the first question was never just whether the medical records have been obtained. The better question is whether the evidence needed to responsibly answer the question in front of you right now has actually been obtained. And that answer can change as the case develops — a record set that's plenty for intake may fall short at the expert-referral stage; a file that's adequate for a focused standard-of-care review may not support a final opinion on causation or damages. This all has to stay tied to whatever decision is actually being made.

We tend to talk about "the medical record" as if it's one unified object. In reality it's almost always a collection of separate systems all operating around the same patient — a physician record, nursing documentation, a lab platform, an imaging archive, a pharmacy system, a patient portal, phone records, a transfer system, an administrative record. Those systems don't always talk to each other cleanly. They can show different timestamps, preserve different information, describe different stages of what's really the same event. A lab interface might show when a result was verified and sent out. The clinical chart might show when that result was filed. An audit trail might show when someone opened the chart, while a later note shows when the result actually got discussed. Each of those sources answers a different question — the lab system establishes availability, the audit trail offers evidence of access, the note documents interpretation or communication, an order shows a decision was made, and the administration record shows whether that decision actually turned into care. The mistake is expecting any one of those sources to answer for all the others. The chart has to be treated as a collection of evidentiary systems, with the real work being figuring out how those systems relate to the patient's journey, and which source can actually be trusted to answer which question.

Patient-identification errors don't show up in every production, and when they do, they can throw off the entire case. A page can get filed under the wrong patient. Records from people with similar names can get combined. Two encounters can get merged incorrectly, or a document can genuinely belong to the right patient but the wrong episode of care entirely. These errors are hard to catch precisely because the information usually looks medically plausible — a chronic condition, a medication, a prior procedure gets accepted as part of this patient's history simply because it happened to show up in the production. Which is why the basic identifiers matter so much: name, date of birth, medical record number, facility, encounter date, whatever else is available, all need to line up.

When they don't, that discrepancy has to get resolved before the information gets used to establish baseline, risk, causation, or damages. A single misfiled record can create a false diagnosis, distort the patient's apparent health before the event, or suggest a treatment history that never actually existed — and that error can then echo through every summary, chronology, expert file, and legal argument built on top of it. Catching this early stops one misplaced document from quietly becoming an accepted part of the patient's story.

Duplicate documentation causes more than administrative annoyance. It changes how evidence actually feels to the person reading it. A statement repeated across several notes can look strongly confirmed. A symptom mentioned many times can start to feel more prominent than it really was. A diagnosis can look firmly established purely because it appears throughout the file. Sometimes those repeated entries really do reflect repeated observation. Sometimes they're just copied text, imported histories, multiple versions of the same document circulating. The difference matters enormously — one observation shouldn't become five independent observations just because it's sitting on five different pages. One disputed history shouldn't harden into established fact simply because it got copied into every later note. Templated findings run into the same trap — a phrase like "alert and oriented" can keep appearing even though nobody actually reassessed the patient's cognition in any meaningful way. None of this means repeated information should get automatically thrown out. It means the reviewer has to work out whether the repetition is new evidence or just repeated language, because without that distinction, duplication can hand weak evidence an authority it never earned.

A signed note doesn't always tell you when the information in it was actually known. Documentation frequently gets finished well after the event it describes — a clinician enters or signs a note later in the day, a discharge summary gets written after the diagnosis and outcome are already clear, an addendum gets tacked on after somebody else raises a concern. None of that makes the documentation unreliable on its own. It does change how the note has to be read. A note signed at six in the evening might describe an assessment that actually happened at two. A summary written after surgery can describe earlier symptoms filtered entirely through the understanding created by the later diagnosis. An addendum can accurately clarify an earlier conversation, or it can quietly smuggle in knowledge that wasn't actually available when the original decision got made. The reviewer has to keep the time of the event, the time the information was first known, the time it got documented, and the time the note was finalized as four separate things — because they can support very different conclusions. A late signature doesn't necessarily mean the care itself was delayed. An early electronic timestamp doesn't necessarily prove the responsible clinician had any meaningful awareness at that moment. The timing of documentation and the timing of clinical awareness have to stay separate from each other.

An order is evidence that a decision was made. It isn't always evidence that the intended care actually happened. A medication can be ordered and then withheld, delayed, refused, or simply never given. A scan can be requested and never performed. A consult can be placed and never completed. A transfer can get initiated while the patient sits at the original facility for hours afterward. That gap can completely change how responsibility gets understood — a professional may have made exactly the right call, and the system around them may simply have failed to carry it out. A treatment might have been delayed because of staffing, verification, availability, patient instability, or the simple absence of an open bed anywhere. Or the order might have been entered only after the clinically important window had already closed. So the evidence has to be followed from decision through implementation, and, where it matters, through the patient's actual response. It's not enough to say antibiotics were ordered — the review may need to establish exactly when they were given, whether the right dose was administered, and what happened afterward. It's not enough to say imaging was requested — the case may hinge on when the study actually happened, when it got interpreted, and when that result actually shaped the care that followed. The order shows intention. The full pathway shows what the patient actually got.

Imaging is often central to a medical case, and the production sometimes contains nothing but the written report. That report matters — it reflects the interpreting professional's conclusion at the time and often carries essential evidence of what got communicated to the treating team. It doesn't necessarily answer every question that comes up later. The original images may be needed to determine whether a subtle finding was actually visible, whether the study itself was technically limited, whether something looks acute or chronic, or whether a comparison image changes the whole read. Later disagreement often concerns the images themselves rather than the wording of the original report — a finding described as absent may simply have been too subtle to catch reasonably at the time, or an expert reviewing it later may conclude it was visible and clinically significant all along. Rereading the written report over and over won't answer those questions. The written report and the original study are related pieces of evidence. They are not the same evidence, and where imaging is central to diagnosis, timing, mechanism, or causation, the original study shouldn't get treated as optional without a real reason — it may need independent review from someone actually qualified to answer that specific imaging question.

Electronic audit evidence can be extremely useful — showing when a chart got opened, when a result got routed, when a document was modified, when a message got acknowledged. It can also be misread badly. Opening a chart doesn't prove every result inside it got reviewed. Access can be automatic, incidental, entirely unrelated to the issue at hand. A timestamp can reflect system activity rather than any meaningful clinical action. And the absence of an electronic record doesn't necessarily prove no communication happened — a phone call, a verbal report, an interaction that never got logged anywhere may well have occurred outside the documented pathway. Audit data has to be read within the design of the system and the normal workflow of the organization that produced it. Used carefully, it can clarify timing and help pin down responsibility. Used carelessly, it manufactures a false sense of certainty. A conclusion that a result was ignored shouldn't rest on the presence or absence of one single timestamp — the review needs to look at how the result was generated, where it got routed, who was supposed to be watching for it, whether the system even tracked access reliably, and what happened afterward. Electronic evidence is only powerful once you actually understand what it means.

Almost every medical production has gaps in it. Not every missing document changes the case. A missing routine note might add almost nothing. A missing nursing flowsheet covering the exact period the patient was deteriorating might be the whole case. An office record from ten years back might be irrelevant to what's actually in dispute. A rehab assessment might be essential to understanding the patient's function and damages after the fact. The real question was never just what's absent — it's what conclusion actually depends on the missing piece. That's where professional judgment starts to matter: a missing record might block an opinion entirely, or it might just limit confidence, leave two plausible readings on the table, call for further digging, or turn out unlikely to change the conclusion at all. That kind of explanation is a lot more useful than a long inventory of every document that isn't there. What the attorney actually needs to know is why the gap matters, and what can or can't be decided because of it. None of this promises a perfect file. It explains how the imperfections actually affect the weight the analysis can carry.

Medical records disagree with each other all the time. A patient might describe symptom onset one way in the emergency department and another way in later testimony. A nursing note might describe severe pain while a physician's note describes the same patient as comfortable. The medication record might show administration at a different time than the narrative documentation suggests. A family member might insist the patient couldn't walk while the chart says the patient ambulated just fine. The temptation, understandably, is to just pick whichever version supports the theory you already like. That's not what careful review does. The conflict has to be named first, then actually examined. Which entry was contemporaneous? Which source had direct knowledge? Were the two accounts even describing the same interval, or the same aspect of the patient's condition? Could both statements actually be true at once — a patient might have walked briefly with assistance while still being unable to walk safely or independently; pain might genuinely have been severe at one assessment and controlled after medication at the next. Sometimes another source resolves the discrepancy. Sometimes it just can't be resolved, and where it can't, that uncertainty has to keep affecting how strong and how certain the final conclusion gets to sound. A polished narrative shouldn't erase real disagreement just because the disagreement makes the case harder to explain cleanly.

Patients and families often remember details that never made it into the chart, and those accounts shouldn't get dismissed just because they aren't clinical documents. They also shouldn't be accepted automatically. A patient may remember the functional reality far more clearly than the medical terminology ever captured it — recalling that they couldn't stand, couldn't breathe comfortably, couldn't stay awake, couldn't take care of themselves, when the chart only records dizziness, shortness of breath, fatigue, or anxiety. A family member may have watched confusion, weakness, or decline that the clinical notes never fully caught. Memory also bends under time, trauma, later knowledge, and the simple fact of having told the story many times since — the final diagnosis can reshape how someone remembers the earlier symptoms without them even realizing it's happening. So the patient's account belongs right alongside the contemporaneous evidence, neither elevated above it nor dismissed beneath it. Where the two differ, that difference deserves a real look — sometimes the patient's account exposes a genuine gap in the documentation, sometimes the chart turns out to be the sturdier foundation, and sometimes, honestly, the truth just stays uncertain. A fair analysis leaves room for all three of those outcomes.

Every material conclusion should be traceable back to its actual source in the evidence. That protects the attorney, the clinician, and the expert alike — and it protects the patient, and the healthcare professionals whose conduct is under examination, too. A claim that the patient stayed hypotensive for four hours should lead directly back to the specific vital signs, times, interventions, and context that support it. A claim that an abnormal result was ignored should point to exactly what the evidence shows about verification, routing, access, communication, and whatever action followed. A claim that the patient was independent before the event should connect to actual records, assessments, or testimony establishing that function. None of this makes every interpretation beyond dispute — reasonable professionals can still land in different places on what the evidence means. It just lets everyone see how that interpretation actually got built. That transparency is essential to any shared language between these professions. Without it, conclusions drift loose from their sources and start getting repeated as though they were simply accepted fact.

Attorneys and clinicians aren't always going to agree, and qualified experts can review the exact same evidence and land somewhere different. That disagreement becomes a lot more useful once the evidentiary foundation underneath it is actually clear. The professionals can then ask whether they're reading the same source differently, relying on different evidence altogether, or giving different weight to a record that's missing. They can work out whether the disagreement is about the clinical meaning of the evidence, the professional obligation that followed from it, or the causal effect on the outcome. Without that foundation, people end up debating conclusions that grew out of entirely different sets of records — one expert reviewed the original imaging while another only ever saw the written report; one clinician saw the medication-administration record while another simply assumed the order proved the treatment happened. None of this eliminates disagreement. It shows you exactly where the disagreement actually starts, which lets the real issue get tested instead of letting professionals talk past each other indefinitely.

All of this can become its own burden if every case gets treated as though it needs a forensic reconstruction of every page and every electronic system. That was never the point. The depth of the work should track the importance of the decision, the complexity of the evidence, and how much uncertainty is actually still in play. A straightforward case might just need basic confirmation that the right patient's records are present, the important sources have been obtained, and the key conclusions can be traced back to something solid. A multi-facility wrongful-death matter might need a detailed reconciliation of versions, timestamps, imaging, communication pathways, and electronic systems. Proportion matters here. The goal was never to manufacture extra work for its own sake — it's to keep incomplete or misunderstood evidence from carrying more weight than it's actually earned. A preliminary decision shouldn't get stalled indefinitely chasing perfect completeness when the evidence already on hand is enough for that limited purpose. At the same time, a final opinion shouldn't rest on a preliminary record set just because getting the rest has turned out to be difficult or expensive. The level of certainty in a conclusion should always match the quality of the foundation it's actually standing on.

A sound evidentiary foundation lets everyone involved know exactly what they're relying on. It can flag missing evidence early, before the theory of the case ever hardens into place. It can stop duplication from being mistaken for confirmation, and reveal whether an apparent delay reflects the actual care, the documentation of it, or just the quirks of an electronic system. It can separate an order from an action, and a written imaging report from the original diagnostic study underneath it. It can show that several professionals are actually discussing the same fact from entirely different sources, or that they've been unknowingly relying on different evidence the whole time. It can also reveal that the available record is stronger than anyone first believed — a communication that looked absent might be sitting in another system, or a disputed treatment might get confirmed through the administration record after all. None of that benefit is about administrative neatness. It's confidence that the analysis that follows is actually starting from the right place.

It's also worth being honest about what checking the record's integrity can't do. No amount of document organization turns an incomplete event into complete certainty. Audit trails get misread. Metadata gets handed more authority than the clinical context actually supports. Chasing perfect completeness can delay a perfectly reasonable preliminary decision without adding anything meaningful to it. There's also a real risk that the record itself starts to matter more than the patient — a beautifully indexed, perfectly reconciled production can still fail completely to explain the patient's function, their experience, or the clinical meaning of the care they received. This is the foundation. It isn't the whole building. The evidence still has to be interpreted clinically. Professional roles still have to be examined. The treatment opportunity still has to be defined, and causation still has to be tested. The most complete record in the world doesn't decide the case by itself.

Here's a case where the record looked complete enough to tell a whole story — and wasn't. A fifty-eight-year-old comes to an emergency department with chest discomfort, nausea, and fatigue. The initial testing is called reassuring, and the patient is discharged. The next morning, they're back with an acute heart attack and significant cardiac damage.

The attorney receives the hospital record — a physician's note, lab results, a reference to an EKG, discharge instructions. The initial theory is that the heart attack was missed at the first visit. At first glance, the production looks like enough to evaluate that. A closer look shows the original EKG tracing is missing entirely — all that's there is an automated interpretation. The lab report shows the final troponin result without ever establishing when it actually became available relative to the discharge. A nursing note mentions continued discomfort shortly before the patient left, and the medication-administration record is nowhere to be found. The patient remembers being told everything was normal, while the discharge instructions describe nonspecific chest pain and tell the patient to come back if it gets worse.

Before the clinical question can even be properly examined, several evidentiary questions have to get answered first. Was the original EKG genuinely reassuring, or did it contain something the automated read missed? Was the final troponin result actually available before discharge? Did the patient keep reporting pain after treatment, and was the response to that treatment ever documented? Was the patient reassessed before leaving? Did the clinical picture call for repeat testing or more observation?

One honest reading shows objective evidence of an evolving cardiac event that existed and simply wasn't acted on — that the patient kept having symptoms, and a reasonable reassessment would have changed the plan entirely. Another honest reading shows studies that really were negative at the time, a patient who improved, and an infarction that developed only after discharge.

The initial set of records looked complete enough to tell a story. It wasn't complete enough to say which story was actually true. That's the whole purpose of paying this much attention to the record's integrity in the first place — it doesn't decide the clinical question before the missing evidence gets found. It tells the attorney whether the foundation already in hand can actually carry the decision being asked of it.

Before law and medicine can share any real understanding of a case, they have to share the evidence first. That doesn't mean receiving the same page count or reading the same summary. It means working from the same reliable evidentiary foundation — confirming the correct patient and encounter, checking that the critical sources are actually present, catching when repeated language has been mistaken for independent confirmation. It means keeping event time separate from documentation time, orders separate from completed care, and electronic access separate from any real clinical awareness. It means keeping conflicts visible instead of smoothing them over, giving the patient's and family's account its proper place, and requiring every material conclusion to trace back to something real. None of it promises a perfect chart — perfect charts basically don't exist. What it gives everyone involved is an honest understanding of what's actually known, what's missing, what's still disputed, and how much weight the evidence on hand can genuinely carry. That's where fair analysis has to begin.

Chapter Nine: Baseline as the First Point of Agreement

Before we can understand what changed, we have to understand what was there beforehand. That sounds almost too obvious to write down, and baseline still ends up being one of the most misunderstood parts of a medical case. The records tell you the patient had diabetes, arthritis, chronic kidney disease, vascular disease, depression, spinal degeneration, a history of falls. All relevant. None of it actually tells you how the patient was living. Someone can carry several chronic conditions and still work, drive, run a household, take care of family, move through their day entirely on their own. Someone else can have a shorter list of diagnoses and already need substantial help. Start with nothing but the list of medical conditions, and you risk misunderstanding both the patient and whatever injury is actually at issue.

Baseline was never just a medical history. It's the condition of the actual person before whatever event is being examined — their symptoms, their treatment, their function, their independence, their vulnerability, how their disease was progressing, and the course their health was probably going to take if none of this had ever happened. That's exactly why baseline can become the first real point of agreement between law and medicine. Before anyone starts arguing about responsibility, causation, or damages, both sides ought to at least be talking about the same patient.

Medical records tend to flatten a patient's past down into a problem list — hypertension, diabetes, osteoarthritis, chronic back pain, coronary artery disease, showing up again and again through the chart. That list can be perfectly accurate and still mislead you badly if it gets used as a stand-in for actually understanding the person. A diagnosis doesn't tell you how severe the condition was. It doesn't tell you whether the symptoms were controlled, whether things were stable or getting worse, or how any of it actually touched the patient's daily life. Most importantly, it doesn't tell you what the patient could actually do. Could they walk without help, work, drive, climb stairs, manage their own medications, live alone, take care of themselves? Could they shop, cook, handle their finances, travel, look after grandchildren, support a spouse? Those are the details that actually make a baseline visible. Skip them, and a medically complex patient can end up described in a way that hides how well they were actually functioning right up until the event. A long diagnosis list can create an impression of serious disability where hardly any functional limitation existed at all. The reverse happens too — a patient with comparatively few recorded diagnoses might already have been frail, cognitively impaired, dependent on others in ways the chart never quite spelled out. The medical labels matter. The life actually lived alongside those labels matters just as much.

The clinician and the attorney tend to use baseline for slightly different reasons. The clinician looks at a patient's prior condition to gauge vulnerability, prognosis, physiological reserve, likely treatment response, and the course the disease probably would have taken without the disputed event. The attorney looks at baseline while weighing injury, causation, damages, life expectancy, and how much of the later loss can fairly be pinned on the conduct in question. Different uses of the same underlying foundation — which means that when the baseline is wrong, both analyses get thrown off at once. An attorney can describe a later disability as entirely new when the patient already had significant impairment going in. A clinician can assume chronic disease explains the whole outcome when the patient had actually been stable and functioning independently right up until the event. A defense can lean hard on the diagnosis list without acknowledging how independent the patient actually was beforehand. A plaintiff can minimize longstanding symptoms or a decline that clearly played some role in the later limitations. Baseline forces everyone to start with the patient as they actually were. That doesn't guarantee agreement about what the event actually did — it just makes sure the disagreement starts from the same comparison point.

One of the most important things to hold onto here is that the comparison was never between this patient and some idealized, perfectly healthy person. It's between the patient before the event and the same patient afterward. Nobody needs to have been disease-free for a later injury to matter — a patient with arthritis can still suffer a genuinely new and significant loss of mobility. A patient with heart disease can sustain additional, avoidable cardiac damage on top of what they already had. A patient with cognitive impairment can suffer a meaningful further decline. Someone who's lived with chronic pain for years can still sustain a new injury that changes their function, their treatment needs, their independence. Prior disease doesn't erase the possibility of new harm. It just changes the question being asked: what was already there? What got worse? What changed in a way that probably wouldn't have happened, at that time, without the event in dispute? That's a far fairer comparison than asking whether the patient had perfect health to begin with, and it dodges two opposite mistakes at once — it stops every later difficulty from getting pinned on the event, and it stops chronic disease from being used to erase real additional harm.

Function usually tells you more than a diagnosis ever could. A patient with lumbar degeneration might have worked a physically demanding job without any restriction at all. Someone with severe arthritis showing up on imaging might have remained entirely active and independent. A patient with chronic lung disease might have needed medication but never supplemental oxygen. Someone with early dementia might have kept living alone with minimal oversight from family. After the event in question, that same person might be unable to return to work, might need home oxygen, might need help with daily activities, might move into supported care. The diagnosis on paper may barely have changed. The person's actual life has changed enormously. Which is why function should never be treated as some secondary detail tacked onto baseline — it's very often the clearest measure of exactly what got lost. Medical records don't always document function consistently or in any real detail, so the clearest evidence often comes from therapy notes, primary-care assessments, employment records, home-health evaluations, family testimony, or simply the patient describing what an ordinary day looked like before all of this happened. A functional baseline is what actually turns a medical history into a real comparison — showing not just what conditions existed, but what those conditions actually meant in the patient's day-to-day life.

Baseline also demands an honest account of whatever symptoms were already present. A patient may have had pain, weakness, shortness of breath, fatigue, confusion, dizziness, or mobility problems before any of this started, and the later claim shouldn't pretend that history away. At the same time, the existence of earlier symptoms shouldn't be stretched to explain everything that followed. The details matter: how often did the symptoms show up? How severe were they? Were they stable, intermittent, worsening? What kept them under control, and how much did they actually interfere with daily life? A patient with occasional back pain is not the same patient as someone with continuous, disabling pain. Someone who used a cane occasionally on long outings is not the same as someone who needed full assistance just to walk. A patient with mild memory trouble living safely at home is not the same as someone who already needed round-the-clock supervision. The diagnosis might use the exact same general label in both cases. The clinical and functional meaning behind that label is completely different, and baseline has to preserve that difference rather than flatten it.

A patient's condition before the disputed event could have been sitting still, or it could have been improving, or declining — and which one of those it was actually matters. A patient with progressive neurological disease may already have been expected to lose function over time regardless. Someone recovering from surgery may have been steadily regaining mobility and independence. A patient with cancer may have had a limited prognosis to begin with. Someone with chronic wounds may already have been deteriorating before the event under review even happened. Baseline was never meant to be a single still photograph. It's a point along a moving path, which means the question isn't only where the patient stood before the event — it's also where they were probably heading. Skip that, and the later outcome gets attributed too broadly or too narrowly. If the patient had been stable for years, an argument that the same severe decline would have happened anyway, right on that same timeline, needs real evidence behind it. If the patient had already entered a period of rapid decline, the disputed event might have worsened that course, sped it up, or shortened whatever period of independence remained — rather than creating the whole problem from scratch. Knowing the direction of travel gives the baseline a realistic sense of time.

Every causation analysis rests on an underlying comparison: what probably would have happened without the disputed event? That's the counterfactual, and baseline is what it's actually built on. When a patient was stable and independent right up until the event, an argument that the same severe decline would have hit at exactly the same moment anyway needs to be backed up with something. When a patient was already deteriorating quickly, the disputed event might have worsened that course, accelerated it, or shortened whatever independent time was left. A patient with a limited life expectancy can still have lost meaningful time, suffered additional pain, needed burdensome treatment, or experienced an avoidable loss of function. The counterfactual has to stay realistic — it shouldn't imagine the patient would have enjoyed perfect health indefinitely, and it shouldn't assume an inevitable, immediate decline just because chronic disease happened to be present. It should track the patient's actual likely course as closely as the evidence allows. Baseline is essential to causation for exactly this reason — without it, the alternative future becomes pure assumption instead of an evidence-based comparison.

Imaging can matter enormously in figuring out whether a later finding is new, chronic, or has simply changed. A later scan can show degeneration, scarring, vascular disease, an old infarction, some other pre-existing abnormality — and without earlier imaging to compare it to, those findings can get pinned incorrectly on the disputed event. It runs the other way too: prior imaging can show a condition existed only in a limited form, while later imaging shows clear progression, a genuinely new injury, or an acute event layered right on top of the chronic disease. The question was never simply whether an abnormality existed beforehand. It's whether the later finding represents the same condition, a worsening of it, a genuinely new feature, an acute injury sitting on top of something chronic, or an entirely unrelated development. That distinction usually needs a qualified imaging review — it shouldn't get assumed from one report, or from the mere appearance of the word "degenerative" somewhere in the chart. Degeneration existing doesn't answer whether trauma, or some other event, materially changed the patient's clinical course. Comparative imaging is what actually shows you what was already there and what changed.

Medication and treatment history can reveal a lot about baseline too. A condition controlled for years on stable treatment tells a different story than one requiring constant medication changes, emergency visits, escalating interventions, or frequent hospitalizations. A new medication can signal recent worsening. Repeated treatment failures can show the patient's condition was already unstable before any of this started. A long gap without care might mean stability, or it might mean poor access, nonadherence, or simply incomplete records — the gap can't be read properly without knowing which. So treatment history has to be actually analyzed rather than just listed out: was the condition well controlled? Were the symptoms stable? Had conservative treatment already failed? Was a procedure already being planned before the event ever happened? Was the patient declining despite entirely appropriate care? Those questions are what help establish what probably would have happened next, and whether the disputed event actually changed that path.

Work history often provides some of the clearest evidence of function you'll find anywhere. A patient who worked regularly before the event and couldn't return afterward has undergone a visible, documentable change — job duties, attendance records, performance reviews, and testimony can all help establish what that patient was physically and cognitively capable of. The same goes for unpaid work. A patient may have cared for a spouse, raised grandchildren, run a household, volunteered, carried real family responsibilities — none of which shows up anywhere in the medical chart, and all of which can be central to understanding both the baseline and the later loss. The point was never to turn every ordinary activity into a line item on a damages claim. It's to actually understand the life this person was living. Someone's ability to work, care for others, run a home, and take part in ordinary life often shows function more clearly than any diagnosis list ever could.

Family members frequently know a patient's daily function better than the medical record ever will. They know whether the patient cooked, drove, managed their own money, climbed stairs, remembered appointments, needed reminders — and they often know whether some quiet decline had already started before the disputed event. That's genuinely valuable, especially when the chart itself is thin on functional detail. It also has to be weighed carefully, because family accounts can be shaped by emotion, by memory, by how serious the later outcome turned out to be, and by everything learned since. Wherever possible, that account should get checked against other evidence — a claim that the patient was fully independent might be backed up by employment records, travel, primary-care notes, home assessments, or it might be challenged by therapy records or earlier notes describing more limitation than the family remembers. The goal was never to accept or reject family evidence automatically. It's to use it in building the most accurate picture available.

A single case can actually have more than one relevant baseline. There might be a long-term health baseline, a functional baseline right before the event in question, a postoperative baseline, or an entirely new baseline established after one injury but before a second one. This matters especially in cases involving several stages of care — a patient enters the hospital seriously ill, improves with treatment, and then suffers a new complication. The right comparison for that later complication may not be how the patient was doing months earlier. It may be how much recovery they'd achieved right before the new event hit. The same goes for a patient who sustains an initial injury, stabilizes, and later suffers harm during rehab or home care — the analysis has to identify which baseline actually fits the question being asked. A single baseline shouldn't get applied mechanically to every stage of a long journey. The comparison has to match the event and the specific difference in outcome being claimed.

A clear baseline can genuinely strengthen a patient's case. It can show that the patient retained real health, function, and independence despite chronic disease. It can demonstrate that a later disability is genuinely new, or that a condition that used to be manageable became substantially worse. Baseline can support a finding of aggravation, acceleration, or lost function. It can show the patient had enough physiological reserve to have actually benefited from timely treatment. It can also reveal that a high-risk patient needed greater vigilance in the first place — vulnerability doesn't necessarily weaken a case. Sometimes vulnerability is exactly why the warning signs deserved closer attention than they got. A patient with limited kidney reserve may be more likely to deteriorate during an infection — and that same vulnerability may be exactly why fluid balance, medication dosing, and lab changes mattered so much more in their case than in someone else's. Baseline can strengthen both the understanding of the injury and the case for why a more careful response was actually required.

The same fair review can just as easily narrow a case. It might show that part of the claimed injury already existed — substantial mobility loss, cognitive impairment, chronic pain, growing care needs, progressive disease, all present before the event. That doesn't end the analysis. It changes the attribution. The disputed care may have caused only part of the later condition. It may have accelerated a decline that was already underway, increased how much assistance the patient needed, or shortened whatever period of independence remained. The case can get narrower this way, and it usually gets more credible for it too — a careful baseline stops the entire post-event condition from getting pinned on the disputed conduct when the evidence really only supports a defined increase in severity or loss. That precision isn't a concession to the other side. It's just responsible causation analysis.

The same baseline fact can pull in more than one direction at once, depending on what you're actually asking of it. A patient with severe kidney disease may have been more likely to deteriorate even with entirely reasonable care — and that same condition may also have demanded more careful attention to medication dosing, lab trends, and fluid balance than a healthier patient would have needed. A patient on blood thinners may have faced a higher risk of bleeding — and that same risk may have called for faster investigation the moment new neurological symptoms showed up. Someone with limited lung reserve may have had a worse prognosis to begin with — and that same vulnerability may have lowered the bar for escalating care the moment their breathing started to worsen. Baseline shouldn't get parked entirely on one side of a case. It can limit causation, raise vulnerability, strengthen the case for vigilance, or do all three at the same time. A fair analysis lets the evidence pull in whichever direction it actually points, instead of only reaching for pre-existing disease when it happens to support whichever theory is already preferred.

Attorneys are often familiar with legal doctrines built around patients who suffer greater harm because of an existing vulnerability. Those doctrines don't remove the need for an actual patient-specific clinical analysis underneath them. The medical work still has to explain what vulnerability existed, how the event actually interacted with it, what harm was genuinely new, what got aggravated, and what probably would have happened without the event at all. The law decides how those findings get treated legally. Clinical Intelligence supplies the medical foundation that legal analysis has to rest on. A broad statement that "the patient was vulnerable" isn't enough on its own — the actual clinical relationship between that vulnerability and the later outcome has to be spelled out, which is exactly what keeps the boundary intact between clinical interpretation and legal judgment.

Experts often get handed records that start just before the disputed event, which can make the later outcome feel disconnected from everything that came before it in the patient's life. A clear baseline helps the expert understand which symptoms were already there, what function was still intact, what disease trajectory was already underway, and what treatment was already planned before any of this started. It also sharpens exactly what outcome difference the expert is actually being asked to weigh in on. An expert shouldn't be asked whether an event caused a disability without first knowing whether some disability already existed, and in what form. The same goes for prognosis — an opinion about shortened survival, increased care needs, or lost recovery potential needs a real sense of what was likely without the disputed event in the picture. Baseline is what lets the expert give an opinion that's actually specific to this patient, and actually defensible.

Clients tend to experience their injury as a hard dividing line — life before felt one way, life after feels completely different — and that experience can be entirely genuine even when real pre-existing disease was present the whole time. The attorney still has to explain how baseline shapes both the medical and legal analysis: some of what came later may be genuinely new, some may be a worsening of problems that already existed, some symptoms may be unrelated altogether, and some causal questions may simply stay uncertain. An honest conversation like that helps a client understand why a case might move forward on aggravation or acceleration rather than complete causation, and why certain damages may need to be separated out from others. Those conversations aren't easy. They're a lot better than letting expectations build around a version of the patient's prior condition that the evidence was never going to support. Baseline is what lets counsel explain the case honestly without ever minimizing what the patient actually went through.

A fair baseline review doesn't go hunting only for evidence of prior disease. It goes looking for evidence of prior function just as hard. It doesn't minimize chronic illness, and it doesn't let chronic illness erase the patient's actual life either. It weighs diagnoses, symptoms, treatment, independence, prognosis, and direction of travel all together, and it's honest about what's confirmed, what's merely reported, and what's still genuinely uncertain. Most importantly, the same baseline needs to hold steady across the whole case — the plaintiff's analysis, the defense analysis, the expert referral, the damages discussion, the conversation with the client shouldn't be quietly describing different versions of who this patient actually was. People can interpret that baseline differently. The underlying facts underneath it need to stay stable and traceable the whole way through. That common foundation is what makes disagreement actually useful, and it's what keeps the patient from shifting shape depending on whatever the argument happens to need that day.

Baseline work can also get out of hand in both directions. A reviewer can collect years of medical history with almost nothing to do with the disputed event, which just buries the important information, drives up cost, and makes the whole case harder to follow. It can also go too narrow

— a short look-back period can miss exactly the pattern of symptoms, treatment, progression, or functional decline that actually controls the analysis. There's no fixed number of years that works for every case. The scope has to follow the actual question. A spinal injury case might need prior imaging and a detailed functional history. A stroke case might need vascular risk factors, earlier neurological symptoms, and evidence of pre-event function. A wrongful-death case might need prognosis, life expectancy, and the course of whatever serious underlying disease was already present. The review should be broad enough to be fair, and focused enough to actually be useful.

Here's an example. A sixty-seven-year-old woman is in a car accident and later reports severe neck pain, arm weakness, and trouble with daily activities. Imaging shows degeneration at multiple levels of her cervical spine.

The defense argues the whole thing is pre-existing. The patient says she had occasional neck stiffness before the accident, but worked full-time, drove, exercised, and needed no help from anyone. Her earlier primary-care records mention intermittent neck discomfort. Prior imaging confirms the degeneration but shows no cord injury. Her employment records show regular attendance, with no earlier therapy, injections, or surgical recommendation anywhere in the file. After the accident, she goes through repeated therapy, gets injections, cuts back her work hours, and eventually has surgery.

Her baseline doesn't support a claim that her spine was completely normal beforehand — the degenerative disease clearly existed. It also doesn't support the conclusion that her later disability was simply the natural continuation of that same condition. The real question is whether the accident materially aggravated a condition that had been manageable up to that point, and changed its actual clinical course.

One honest reading shows pre-existing degeneration that was asymptomatic, or well controlled, followed by a real increase in symptoms, treatment, and functional limitation after the collision. Another honest reading shows a disease that was already progressing, symptoms that were already climbing before the accident, and surgery that probably would have become necessary regardless of what happened on the road that day. The fair conclusion here could be complete causation, aggravation, acceleration, temporary worsening, or no material change tied to the event at all. Baseline is what lets every one of those possibilities actually get tested. Without it, one side describes the patient as perfectly healthy and the other describes the whole condition as pre-existing, and neither version reflects the actual person who existed before any of this happened.

Before law and medicine can agree on what an event caused, they have to reach a reliable understanding of who the patient actually was beforehand. Not a diagnosis list. Not some idealized version of perfect health. The real person — the symptoms they already lived with, the treatment they already needed, the work and daily responsibilities they carried, the independence they still had, and the direction their health was already moving in. Baseline is the comparison every later conclusion in the case actually depends on. Without it, you end up attributing too much, or too little, or simply misunderstanding the injury altogether. The patient's journey didn't begin at the disputed event. The analysis shouldn't either.

Chapter Ten: Imaging and Objective Evidence

Imaging tends to carry an unusual kind of authority in a medical case. A scan produces an actual picture, the report is written in confident technical language, and the finding can feel fixed in a way that symptoms, memory, and professional judgment never quite are. That apparent objectivity can genuinely help — imaging can confirm an injury exists, show how it progressed, tell an acute finding apart from chronic disease, clarify the anatomy, or explain a change in function. It can support the timing of an event and help pin down the mechanism behind it. The trouble starts the moment we ask an image to answer a question it was never capable of answering on its own.

A scan can show a hemorrhage, a fracture, an infarction, a spinal abnormality, an infection, a tumor, a postoperative complication. What it usually can't establish on its own is the exact moment the condition began, whether it could have been prevented, whether some other professional should have caught it sooner, or what would have happened to the patient under a different course of care. Getting to those conclusions means putting the image back into the patient's actual journey — the timing matters, the reason the study was ordered matters, the type and quality of the exam matters, the information given to whoever interpreted it matters, and so does the patient's symptoms and exam findings at that exact point. Earlier studies, how the patient responded to treatment, and whatever happened later can all shift what a given image actually means. In a lot of cases, the original images matter every bit as much as the written report describing them. Imaging is at its most useful when it's treated as evidence inside the case — not as the whole case by itself.

The written radiology report is genuinely important evidence — it records what the interpreting physician saw and concluded at the moment of the study, and it can show what clinical history they were given, what comparison studies were on hand, and whether any technical limitations affected the exam. But the report isn't the image. It's one qualified professional's interpretation of that image, and that distinction matters a great deal once a case turns on whether some subtle finding was actually visible, whether the study itself was technically adequate, or whether a later reviewer believes an abnormality was already sitting there the whole time. A later expert might agree entirely with the original report. Another might identify a finding nobody described the first time around. A third might believe the finding is visible in hindsight but was too subtle or nonspecific to have demanded a different read back when it actually mattered. Those are three genuinely different opinions, not variations on the same one. The attorney needs to know precisely which of those is actually being offered — a broad claim that an earlier scan was "missed" doesn't tell you whether the finding was actually present, how visible it was, whether a reasonable interpreter should have caught it, or whether catching it would even have changed the patient's treatment. The image can open that inquiry. It can't finish it alone.

A scan captures the body at one particular moment. Disease keeps going both before and after that moment, which is easy to forget once you're staring at a clean, definitive-looking picture. An early study can be genuinely normal. It can also simply be too early to show a condition that only becomes visible later. A later image can show extensive injury without ever pinning down the exact hour that injury actually developed, or the moment it became irreversible. This matters enormously in cases involving an evolving stroke, an infection, internal bleeding, ischemia, a spinal injury, a postoperative complication, certain cancers. The later image can make the earlier symptoms much easier to understand in hindsight — it doesn't automatically prove the same finding was present, or even visible, on the earlier study. The analysis has to keep what may have been happening biologically separate from what the available imaging could reasonably have shown at the time. A condition can have existed before it was detectable at all. It can also have been visible earlier and simply overlooked. Those are two very different scenarios needing two very different kinds of evidence and expert analysis — and a dramatic later scan shouldn't be allowed to quietly rewrite the earlier image without a qualified professional actually looking at both.

Not every imaging exam answers every clinical question. A plain X-ray might be exactly right for one concern and useless for another. A non-contrast CT might rule certain emergencies in or out while remaining limited for other conditions entirely. Ultrasound can be valuable, and it's also sensitive to anatomy, technique, who's operating the machine, and exactly what question is being asked. MRI can show the brain, spinal cord, soft tissue, or musculoskeletal detail far more clearly, and it isn't always immediately available or appropriate in every setting. The fact that some imaging got done doesn't establish that the relevant condition was actually fully evaluated. The review has to ask what condition was even being considered, which study got chosen, and whether that study was capable of answering the question in front of the clinician — and it may matter whether contrast, additional views, comparison studies, or a different modality altogether were actually needed. An exam can have been technically limited. An original study can have answered the question being asked at the time and simply become insufficient once the patient's condition changed. These are normally questions for real clinical and specialty input — an attorney shouldn't assume a study was adequate just because one was done, and a reviewing clinician shouldn't assume a more advanced study was obviously required just because it later happened to reveal the diagnosis. The real issue is whether the imaging choice was reasonable given the patient and the information available at that stage of the journey.

Radiologists don't read images in a vacuum — the clinical information sent along with the study can shape what gets noticed and how the findings get understood. A request that says "rule out fracture" points attention somewhere different than one describing progressive weakness after trauma. A scan ordered for expected postoperative discomfort gets approached differently than one ordered because the patient has a fever, a climbing heart rate, and concern for a leak. None of that means an interpreting professional gets to ignore abnormalities outside whatever was specifically flagged — it just means the quality and specificity of the clinical information genuinely shapes the interpretation. Sometimes the problem was never really in how the image got read. It was in the question that accompanied it. The requesting clinician may never have communicated the patient's most significant symptoms — maybe those symptoms hadn't developed yet, or maybe the imaging department only ever got a brief note through some limited electronic field. So the attorney has to look at both the study and the clinical information that traveled with it, because a later expert reviewing the complete record often has vastly more context than the original interpreter ever had — and that gap has to stay visible when anyone judges how reasonable that original read actually was.

The phrase "no acute finding" shows up constantly in imaging reports. It can sound reassuring, and what it actually means still depends entirely on the study and the question behind it. It can mean no acute abnormality showed up within the limits of that specific exam. It doesn't always mean every serious condition got ruled out. The attorney should ask what the study could reliably detect, what sat outside its sensitivity, and whether the patient's later course called for a different kind of evaluation. At the same time, a normal study shouldn't get dismissed just because the eventual diagnosis turned out to be serious — a genuinely reassuring image can be exactly what supports the reasonableness of the original plan, and the patient's later deterioration may simply reflect progression that wasn't visible yet. Both possibilities have to stay on the table. A normal early study can be limited and still have been read entirely reasonably. It can also have been falsely reassuring, if the wrong study got picked or the clinical picture called for more investigation regardless of that one result. The phrase sitting in the report can't answer either question by itself.

A single study can be genuinely hard to make sense of without knowing what came before it. Prior imaging can show that an abnormality was longstanding, stable, chronic — a lesion, a fracture, a disc problem, an old infarct, a degenerative change, a vascular finding that existed well before the event in question. It can just as easily show that the later study contains something genuinely new, or clear progression from what was there before. This matters enormously in cases involving trauma, spinal disease, degenerative conditions, prior stroke, tumors, vascular disease, chronic wounds. The question was never simply whether an abnormality existed beforehand. The analysis has to determine whether the later image shows a meaningful change, and whether that change actually lines up with the patient's symptoms and loss of function. A patient might have had cervical degeneration for years and stayed active and independent the whole time — and after some event, the imaging shows no dramatic structural change while the patient experiences a real jump in symptoms and functional loss. Another patient might report similar symptoms while comparison imaging reveals a clear, acute injury. Imaging and baseline have to be weighed together. Neither one should get to decide the whole case on its own.

Imaging gets called objective evidence for good reason — the image itself exists independently of the patient's memory or a reviewer's narrative. Interpreting it still takes real professional judgment. Qualified specialists can disagree about whether a subtle finding is even present, whether it's acute, whether it explains the patient's symptoms, whether it should have been caught earlier, and whether catching it would have changed the treatment opportunity at all. That disagreement doesn't make imaging unreliable. It means the evidence has to be read within its actual limits — which is just as true of every other form of "objective" evidence. Lab values, vital signs, pathology findings, device data, monitoring traces can all look precise on the page, and their real significance still depends on the baseline, the timing, the trend, how technically reliable the measurement was, and the clinical context around it. A number can be exact and its meaning can still be genuinely uncertain. Objective evidence narrows some kinds of uncertainty. It never removes the need for someone qualified to interpret it.

A scan can clearly show a hemorrhage, an infarction, a fracture, a spinal abnormality, organ injury, a postoperative complication — and still not explain why any of it happened. A hemorrhage can be related to trauma, medication, vascular disease, surgery, high blood pressure, or something else entirely. A fracture can be traumatic, pathological, or shaped by underlying bone disease. A spinal finding can be degenerative, acute, or some mix of both. A postoperative fluid collection can be an expected part of healing, an infection, a leak, bleeding, or some other complication. Figuring out the cause takes the clinical history, the mechanism, the timing, the exam, the lab findings, and the wider record — not just the picture. This is one of the places law and medicine often look like they're disagreeing when they're actually just answering different questions. The attorney looks at the image and sees proof a serious injury occurred. The clinician can agree completely with that and still be genuinely uncertain about when it developed, what caused it, or how much of the outcome traces back to whatever's being disputed. Those two positions aren't actually inconsistent — the image can establish that an injury exists without establishing mechanism, and without establishing legal causation either.

A treatment or procedure can be biologically connected to something showing up on imaging without that connection proving the care was unreasonable. A catheter can cause vascular injury despite entirely appropriate technique. A surgical procedure can be followed by a well-recognized complication. Anticoagulation can contribute to bleeding even when giving it was the right call. A fall can fracture a bone in a patient with severe osteoporosis despite reasonable precautions being in place. The image can support the causal relationship between an event and an injury while the standard-of-care question stays completely separate: how did the event actually happen? Was the known risk managed reasonably? Should some different precaution, assessment, or response have been used? Was the complication recognized and treated properly once it developed? Imaging can help answer part of that. It shouldn't be allowed to collapse causation and professional responsibility into one single question.

Some imaging findings help you figure out whether an injury is acute, subacute, evolving, established, or chronic — genuinely useful information. That estimate shouldn't get more precise than the images, or the underlying science, actually allow. A radiologist might be able to say a finding looks recent without being able to name the exact hour it started. A later image can show progression compared to an earlier one without ever establishing exactly when, between those two studies, the meaningful change actually happened. A legal theory might depend on a narrow window of time — and when the imaging only supports a range, the analysis has to stay a range too. Precision shouldn't get manufactured just because more precision would help the case. The image gets to establish what it can actually support. Nothing more.

Sometimes the important question is why imaging never happened at all. That inquiry has to stay specific to this patient — not every symptom calls for imaging, and the decision to image involves weighing radiation, contrast risk, delay, cost, incidental findings, and whether some other reasonable way to assess things was already available. Plenty of conditions get evaluated first through an exam, lab testing, observation, or how the patient responds to treatment. The later diagnosis doesn't prove imaging was required at that first visit. The reviewer has to ask what was actually known at the time, which serious conditions were reasonably being considered, and whether the patient's exam and response to treatment supported a lower-risk approach. The patient may have been improving. The early symptoms may genuinely not have justified imaging yet. New findings may only have shown up later. Often the sharper question isn't whether imaging was needed immediately — it's whether a failure to improve, a return visit, or new symptoms developing should have changed the plan. The absence of imaging becomes meaningful exactly at the point where the patient's developing journey creates a genuine, reasonable need to look further.

A prior normal study can be reassuring, and it shouldn't end the inquiry the moment the patient's condition actually changes. Repeat imaging can become appropriate once symptoms worsen, new neurological findings appear, treatment fails, the patient comes back, objective trends get worse, or the original exam turns out to have been technically limited. The question was never whether repeating the study would eventually have found the diagnosis — it's whether the patient's changing course created a reasonable need for another look, which depends on how the earlier result actually relates to the later clinical findings. A normal scan obtained before any deterioration can remain entirely reasonable. Continuing to lean on that same normal scan after the patient develops new, significant findings may not be. Repeat imaging is really just part of reassessment — it reflects the same basic principle running through so much of this: a reasonable first decision still has to stay responsive to a patient whose condition keeps changing.

An abnormal image doesn't always explain the patient's actual disability. A dramatic degenerative finding may have caused almost no functional limitation before the event. A subtle lesion can produce serious weakness, cognitive change, pain, or lost independence. So imaging has to be weighed alongside the symptoms, the exam findings, the treatment, the functional change, and how the patient responded over time — which matters enormously in personal-injury and chronic-pain cases, where the radiographic findings and the lived disability often don't line up neatly at all. The absence of a dramatic image doesn't prove the patient has no injury. The presence of a dramatic abnormality doesn't prove the disputed event caused every symptom or limitation the patient later reports. That clinical relationship has to actually get established. The image shows the anatomy. The patient's journey shows what that anatomy actually meant in their life.

Not every clinician should be interpreting original imaging on their own. A reviewer can recognize that imaging is central to a case and identify exactly what questions need answering, while the formal interpretation stays with someone actually qualified to give it. What kind of expertise that takes depends on the issue — a neuroradiologist for a subtle brain or spinal finding, a musculoskeletal radiologist for an orthopedic injury, a surgeon to explain how the image connects to operative decisions, a neurologist to tie the findings to the patient's symptoms, treatment eligibility, and prognosis. This whole approach helps identify the imaging question and the professional who should actually be answering it. It doesn't remove the need for either one. That boundary matters, because being familiar with medical records doesn't give anyone the authority to render a specialist imaging opinion. The goal was always to improve expert selection, never to substitute for qualified review.

When experts disagree about imaging, it helps enormously to pin down exactly where that disagreement actually lives. They might disagree about whether a finding was even visible on the original study. They might agree it was visible and disagree about whether it was clinically significant. They might agree it was significant and disagree about whether a reasonable interpreter should have caught it at the time. They might agree recognition was possible and still disagree about whether catching it would have changed the treatment or the outcome. Those are four completely different disputes wearing the same general label of "disagreement." Telling an attorney that the radiologists simply disagree doesn't tell them much of anything — the disagreement has to be tied to the actual decision it affects. If the dispute is about visibility, the original images and technical quality are what matter. If it's about recognizability, the professional standard and how subtle the finding was matter. If it's about significance, the patient's symptoms and clinical context matter. If it's about outcome, treatment opportunity and causation need their own separate examination. Defining the disagreement this precisely is what keeps four different questions from collapsing into one muddled one.

Artificial intelligence and other advanced imaging tools are showing up more and more to help with detection, prioritization, measurement, segmentation. These tools can genuinely improve speed and consistency. They can also produce false positives, false negatives, and findings that still need a professional to actually interpret them. An automated flag doesn't establish that the treating clinician should have reached the same conclusion — especially when that technology wasn't even available, or in use, at the time the care was given. A later algorithmic analysis shouldn't automatically get treated as evidence of what the historical professional standard actually was. Technology can help a reviewer take a second look. It shouldn't get to rewrite what was reasonably available, expected, or recognizable back when the decision was actually made. Human interpretation, verifying the source, staying within professional scope, and keeping the historical context intact all still matter just as much as they ever did.

Imaging can supply some of the strongest evidence in an entire medical case. It can confirm an injury, show its progression, tell a new finding apart from chronic disease, clarify the anatomy, support the mechanism, flag an evolving abnormality, explain a treatment decision, help define a prognosis. It can offer objective support exactly where symptoms or recollections are in genuine dispute. It can also protect a professional when the earlier study really was reassuring, or when the condition simply wasn't visible yet. The strength of imaging lives in what it actually shows — not in what either side hopes it proves. That's exactly why original studies, qualified interpretation, comparison imaging, and clinical context matter as much as they do.

It's just as important to guard against giving imaging too much authority. A later study can make the earlier course look obvious in hindsight. A written report can get treated as though it captured every relevant observation. A subtle finding can get described as an obvious miss even when reasonable readers might genuinely disagree. A chronic abnormality can get pinned on a new event without anyone pulling comparison imaging. A visible injury can get waved around as though it were proof of negligence all by itself. None of those conclusions should ever be automatic. The image has to stay tethered to time, to symptoms, to baseline, to professional role, to treatment opportunity, and to qualified interpretation. Imaging should clarify the patient's journey. It shouldn't be allowed to pull the analysis away from it.

Here's an example. A seventy-two-year-old comes to an emergency department with a severe headache, nausea, and a brief period of confusion. A non-contrast CT of the head is reported as showing no acute intracranial abnormality. The patient improves with medication and is discharged. The next day, they're back with a worsening headache and neurological changes, and a repeat scan shows a subarachnoid hemorrhage.

The first allegation is that the original scan was misread. That might be true, and it might not be the only issue in the case. The original images need review by someone actually qualified to give an opinion on them, and that first report has to be weighed alongside whatever clinical information radiology actually received. The patient's exam, risk factors, response to treatment, and discharge plan all matter here too.

A later expert might identify a subtle abnormality on that first study. The next question is whether the finding was visible and significant enough that a reasonable radiologist should have caught it at the time. And even if the original scan really was reasonably read as negative, another question remains: did the patient's presentation call for further investigation, observation, a different type of study, or firmer return precautions, regardless of that negative result? The causation question sits apart from all of that. Would an earlier diagnosis probably have prevented the later neurological injury? Was effective treatment actually available? Had the bleeding already started, such that the outcome would only have been reduced rather than prevented outright?

One honest reading shows the abnormality was actually visible on the original scan, or that the clinical presentation called for more evaluation regardless of what the report said. Another honest reading shows a first study that really was negative, a patient who improved appropriately, and a hemorrhage that developed, or became visible, only later. The image is central to this case. It is not the whole case.

An image can show something words simply can't. It can confirm an injury, reveal how it progressed, and bring real clarity to a disputed clinical course. It can also tempt everyone involved into believing the picture answers every question sitting in front of them. It doesn't. The image has to be placed in time and measured against whatever came before it. It has to be tied to the patient's symptoms, exam, treatment, function, and outcome. It has to be interpreted by the right professional, and any disagreement about it needs to be defined at the exact point where it actually arises. Most of all, the image has to be allowed to prove only what it can actually prove. Imaging is very often one of the strongest pieces of evidence in the whole case. It becomes strongest exactly when everyone understands its limits.

Chapter Eleven: Time, Recognizability, and the Patient Journey

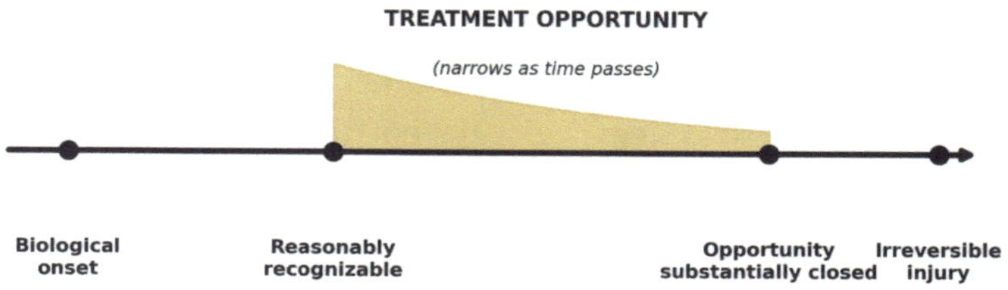

Figure 11.1 — Recognizability, treatment opportunity, and irreversible injury over time

Time is usually the first thing anyone looks for in a medical case. How long did the patient wait? How long before someone ordered the test? How much time passed before treatment started, before the transfer happened, before surgery, before a specialist actually got involved? Those questions matter, and time on its own doesn't tell you whether the care was reasonable or whether some delay actually changed the outcome. The harder question is when the patient's condition became recognizable for what it actually was — or at least concerning enough that a different response became necessary. That point is almost never as simple as the first symptom, or the final diagnosis.

A disease can be developing well before it's even possible to identify. A patient can show up with symptoms that are common and completely nonspecific. Early exams and tests can be entirely reassuring, and the initial plan can be perfectly reasonable given everything anyone knew at that moment. The real problem often shows up later, when the patient doesn't improve, new findings appear, or the original explanation stops fitting the course things are actually taking. Which is exactly why a meaningful timeline can't be built out of nothing but dates and times. It has to show when the meaning of the evidence actually changed.

When a patient experiences a serious outcome, it's natural to look back to the earliest complaint and start measuring the delay from right there. Sometimes that's the right call. Other times it paints a genuinely misleading picture. A headache can start hours before an intracranial hemorrhage becomes clinically apparent. Abdominal discomfort can be present well before there's enough evidence to tell a dangerous postoperative complication apart from an ordinary recovery. Fatigue and weakness can show up before sepsis without making an infection reasonably recognizable yet. A patient can have intermittent chest discomfort before the clinical picture is concerning enough to demand emergency intervention. The first symptom tells you when the patient's own experience began. It doesn't always tell you when some other professional response became necessary. The meaningful starting point might be the first visit — or it might be the first abnormal finding, the first change in function, the first failure to improve, or the patient's return after an earlier encounter. It might be a new result that raises the level of concern, or the moment several smaller findings finally add up to a recognizable pattern. Wherever that starting point ends up, it should be chosen because the evidence actually supports it — not because it happens to produce the longest possible delay on paper.

Plenty of medical conditions exist biologically well before they can actually be diagnosed. A stroke can be evolving before any focal neurological finding shows up. An infection can already be present before the patient develops a pattern that demands escalation. A postoperative leak can have started before the pain, fever, climbing heart rate, and dropping urine output make the complication obvious. Cancer can exist before it's reliably detectable through symptoms, imaging, or lab testing. The biological event and the clinical event are related to each other. They aren't the same thing, and that distinction is what protects a review from hindsight — it stops you from concluding that because a disease was later found to exist, it must have been recognizable at every earlier point along the way. It also guards against the opposite mistake: early uncertainty shouldn't get used to excuse care after the condition had clearly become a great deal more apparent. The real work is finding the point where the case actually moved from uncertainty that could reasonably be managed into risk that demanded a different response.

A condition rarely becomes recognizable in one dramatic instant. More often, its meaning builds gradually. A patient starts with mild abdominal pain. Later, the pain increases. The heart rate starts climbing, mobility drops off, urine output falls. Any single one of those findings might not be enough to change the plan on its own. Taken together, they can form a pattern that simply can't be explained away as routine recovery anymore. That pattern is often scattered across different parts of the record — a nurse notes increasing discomfort, a therapy note shows reduced participation, the medication record shows repeated rescue doses, the labs start trending the wrong way. No single entry may ever come out and say the patient is deteriorating. The patient's actual journey does. Bringing those findings together and asking when the combined pattern became significant enough to demand reassessment, escalation, more testing, or a change in treatment — that's where a chronology stops being a list of events and starts actually showing the development of risk.

A professional doesn't always need to know the final diagnosis before acting becomes necessary. The exact cause can stay uncertain while the level of danger is already clear. A patient may not yet have a confirmed pulmonary embolism, and sudden shortness of breath with falling oxygen levels can still demand urgent assessment. A patient may not yet have a confirmed intracranial hemorrhage, and worsening consciousness after a head injury can still demand repeat imaging. A patient may not have culture-confirmed infection, and falling blood pressure with confusion and rising oxygen needs can still demand escalation. This matters because so many cases get framed too narrowly as a failure to diagnose, when the real issue is whether the professional recognized that the patient was no longer safe under the existing plan. Diagnosis is often the eventual endpoint. Recognizing the danger usually comes first — and the actual obligation may simply be to investigate, watch more closely, get a consult, transfer, or change the plan, well before anyone has landed on the final diagnosis.

It's tempting to assume that if a serious diagnosis wasn't caught at the first visit, the initial decision must have been wrong. That's not always true. The patient may have shown up early, when the symptoms were genuinely nonspecific. The exam may have been reassuring, and the testing entirely appropriate for what anyone knew at the time. The initial treatment may have produced real improvement, making discharge, observation, or a conservative approach entirely reasonable in that moment. A reasonable first decision doesn't guarantee the whole course that followed stayed reasonable. The obligation to keep thinking doesn't end the moment the first plan gets chosen — the patient may fail to improve, may come back with new symptoms, may produce a result that raises the level of concern, or a family member may report a real functional change nobody had seen before. The question then becomes whether the plan actually got revisited once the evidence changed. In a lot of these cases, the real failure was never the original decision. It was continuing to lean on that decision after it stopped fitting the patient in front of them.

Improvement is usually expected after treatment, and when it doesn't show up, that absence itself becomes clinically meaningful. A patient treated for dehydration should generally show some response. A patient given medication for a benign explanation of pain should be expected to improve enough to function safely. A postoperative patient should stay within an expected range of recovery, even with some ongoing discomfort. When the patient doesn't respond the way anyone anticipated, the original explanation may need a second look. None of this makes a failure to improve automatic proof of negligent care — some illnesses just don't respond quickly, some treatments take time, some patients stay unwell despite entirely appropriate management. Even so, a lack of the expected response is still new information. It can be exactly the point where the risk shifts and another assessment becomes necessary. The absence of improvement can carry just as much weight as the appearance of a brand-new abnormal finding.

A patient can feel better without actually being better. Pain medication can ease discomfort while the underlying condition keeps progressing underneath it. Fluids can improve blood pressure briefly while an infection or a bleed keeps getting worse. Supplemental oxygen can improve the saturation reading even as respiratory failure grows more severe. Sedating medication can make a patient look calmer while making neurological deterioration much harder to spot. Temporary improvement can support the reasonableness of an initial plan. It shouldn't be treated as proof the danger has passed. The real questions are what actually improved, whether that improvement held, and whether real function came back. Did the patient need less support, or did the underlying trend simply become less visible for a while? The answer might show real recovery. It might also show that treatment was temporarily masking the very sign that had drawn attention to the problem in the first place.

Reassessment is often where time and professional responsibility actually meet. A patient's condition isn't static — a decision that was entirely reasonable at ten in the morning may not be reasonable anymore by two in the afternoon if the patient hasn't improved, or has developed something new. A meaningful timeline needs to show more than the initial assessment and the eventual outcome. It has to show whether the patient actually got reassessed after treatment, after a new result, after a reported change, after a return visit, after a failed discharge plan, after a worsening trend. The absence of reassessment can matter enormously, and the quality of the reassessment matters just as much. A brief note saying "no change" doesn't necessarily mean the clinically important problem actually got looked at again — a patient treated for dizziness needs their gait reassessed, not just confirmation that the nausea improved. A patient with worsening confusion needs an actual neurological reassessment, not just another routine set of vital signs. Reassessment has to be aimed at whatever risk actually remains.

Communication creates some of the trickiest timing questions in any medical case. A nurse may recognize deterioration before the physician even knows about it. A lab may release a result before it ever reaches the responsible team. A patient may leave a phone message that doesn't get reviewed until much later. A consultant may get a referral and not understand how urgent the request actually is. The record can show that communication happened without ever documenting what was actually said. It can show the content of a message without establishing when the person receiving it actually understood its significance. So the timeline has to keep separate: when a finding occurred, when it got documented, when it got communicated, who received it, and when action actually followed. A delay can happen in recognition, in communication, in decision-making, or in implementation — those are genuinely different kinds of delay, they can belong to entirely different professionals or systems, and they can carry very different clinical and legal weight. A case that gets described broadly as "delayed treatment" might actually involve timely recognition followed by a communication failure. Another might involve prompt communication followed by delayed implementation, simply because the necessary resources weren't there. The actual pathway is what matters.

A result can sit inside an electronic system for a while before anyone actually reviews it. An imaging report can get finalized before the treating professional ever reads it. A lab result can land in a shared queue without ever getting assigned to a specific person. A consult note can get filed after the patient has already left the building. Information existing somewhere in the system doesn't necessarily mean it was reasonably known to whoever was responsible for acting on it — that depends entirely on the workflow. Who was actually supposed to be watching for that result? Did an alert fire? Was the result flagged as urgent? Did the system require someone to acknowledge it? Was responsibility clearly assigned to one person, or did the information just sit in some shared space everyone could technically access and nobody specifically owned? The significance of any timestamp depends on how the healthcare process was actually designed to work. An electronic time tells you when something happened inside the system. It doesn't automatically tell you what any particular professional actually knew.

Sometimes the risk gets recognized and treatment still doesn't start right away. The patient may need transfer to another facility. A specialist may not be available, or there may be no appropriate bed anywhere. Consent may take time. The patient may be too unstable for transport, or a medication may need verification before it can be given. Practical realities can genuinely limit how fast the preferred response is able to happen —

which doesn't make every delay automatically reasonable. It means the timeline has to show what actually happened in the gap between recognition and treatment. Were reasonable steps taken? Was the urgency actually communicated? Were alternatives considered, and was the patient properly supported while everyone waited? Did the delay come from the patient's own condition, from resource availability, from how the system was designed, or from someone simply failing to act? Those distinctions carry real clinical and legal weight — an unavoidable delay in transfer looks completely different from a delay caused by nobody ever placing the request. A treatment that genuinely couldn't start safely looks completely different from one that was simply overlooked.

Time-sensitive treatments tend to get discussed in terms of general windows, and those windows are useful without settling every individual case. A patient can arrive within a widely accepted window and still be ineligible because of imaging findings, bleeding risk, other health conditions, prior function, or some other contraindication. Another patient can remain eligible later than expected because their clinical picture and imaging look different. The question was never simply whether treatment was generally available somewhere in the world. It's whether the treatment was actually available to this patient at the relevant moment — which usually takes more than pointing at a guideline or a standard time range. It often needs a specialist to actually weigh the patient's symptoms, imaging, labs, risks, and expected benefit. General treatment windows help frame the inquiry. Patient-specific eligibility is what determines whether a real opportunity actually existed.

A causation analysis needs more than the point where a different response should have happened — it also needs to know when the opportunity to make a meaningful difference ended, or shrank substantially. The treatment opportunity lives somewhere between those two points. That interval can be clear, or it can stay genuinely uncertain. It can narrow gradually instead of slamming shut at one precise instant. The evidence might support that earlier action probably would have prevented the whole injury. It might instead support only a reduction in severity. Some harm might already have happened while further harm remained preventable. In another case, the opportunity might have closed before the alleged failure even took place. The timing analysis has to stay honest enough to allow for any of those outcomes — a treatment window shouldn't get treated as an all-or-nothing line unless the patient-specific evidence actually supports reading it that way. The benefit can fade gradually over time rather than vanishing at some single, universally fixed moment.

A delay might last six hours on paper, while the causally important part of it is much shorter. The first two hours might occur before the condition is even reasonably recognizable. Over the next two, intervention might remain highly beneficial. By the final two, the injury might already be largely set, even though treatment is still needed at that point. Calling the entire six hours a harmful delay can overstate the case. Treating none of that interval as meaningful, just because the earliest symptoms were uncertain, can understate it just as badly. The timeline needs to identify the stretch that actually matters — the point where recognizability, professional responsibility, treatment opportunity, and causation all meet each other. The legal significance of time depends not just on how much time passed, but on what was actually knowable, and actually possible, during each piece of that interval.

Healthcare professionals don't all see the same sequence of events. The nurse might observe the patient repeatedly while the physician only checks in at intervals. The radiologist sees the imaging and not whatever's happening at the bedside. A specialist might only receive whatever made it into the referral. The patient and their family might witness a functional decline that no single professional ever sees continuously. Which means a pattern can become obvious in hindsight, once you look at the complete record, even though no individual professional ever saw the whole thing unfold in real time. So the analysis has to ask more than whether the pattern existed — it has to work out which parts of that pattern were actually available to the specific person or system whose conduct is being examined. A nurse may have observed several changes and had no authority to order treatment. A physician may have received only one of those observations. A consultant may have gotten an incomplete account that never conveyed the urgency visible across the full record.

Reconstructing the complete journey is necessary. Loading the combined knowledge of every professional onto any one of them individually is not. That's the difference between a fair reconstruction and collective hindsight dressed up as one.

Patients and families often experience delay as waiting — they remember how long it took before someone actually listened, called back, ordered the test, explained the result, arranged the transfer. That experience matters. It can reveal communication failures, real distress, stretches of deterioration the chart never quite captures. The clinical and legal analysis still needs more than that experience alone. The length of the wait has to get connected to what was actually happening medically, what was known, what could reasonably have been done, and whether the delay actually changed the outcome. A wait can be genuinely distressing without being causative. It can also look completely ordinary in the chart while being clinically significant underneath. Both of those perspectives deserve real weight — the patient's experience helps you understand the journey, the clinical evidence determines what the passage of time actually meant medically, and counsel works out how all of that affects the case.

Once the final diagnosis is known, the earlier pattern can look obvious. A later expert can point to subtle findings that fit the diagnosis perfectly — which doesn't necessarily mean the treating professional should have made that same connection back when it mattered. The review has to ask whether those signs were specific, clearly documented, and available together at the time. Were other explanations reasonable back then? Did the treating professional have the same information the later expert now has, including later imaging, later labs, and the outcome everyone already knows? A fair analysis shouldn't ignore subtle evidence just because it's inconvenient. It also shouldn't let later certainty quietly rewrite earlier uncertainty. The question is what a reasonable professional could and should have recognized with the information they actually had at the time — a very different standard from asking what the record seems to show once you already know how it ends.

Protecting against hindsight shouldn't turn into a justification for doing nothing after the evidence has clearly changed. Medicine often starts in genuine uncertainty. It shouldn't stay there once the patient's condition grows more concerning. A diagnosis can still be uncertain while the need to escalate is already obvious — a professional may not know exactly what's wrong and may still know that the patient is no longer safe for discharge, casual observation, or routine follow-up. What matters is finding that point — respecting genuine uncertainty while still asking when the uncertainty itself became dangerous. The failure, sometimes, isn't that the final diagnosis stayed unknown. It's that the patient stayed on a plan that no longer matched how much risk they were actually carrying. That distinction alone can change the entire theory of a case.

A useful clinical timeline should help the reader understand the patient's baseline, how the symptoms started and progressed, and what information was actually available at each stage. It should show the working explanation, the treatment given, and how the patient responded. It should show new findings as they emerged, and the pathway those findings actually traveled through to reach someone. It should show the point where the original plan needed reconsidering, whatever intervention remained available, and the stretch of time during which avoidable harm probably occurred. Not every event deserves the same amount of space — the timeline should slow down exactly where the case becomes clinically important. A handful of critical hours might need painstaking reconstruction while months of routine care get a couple of sentences. The point was never to log every tick of the clock. It's to show when the clinical meaning actually changed.

A clinically reconstructed timeline can bring real clarity to a case that looks, at first, either too simple or hopelessly tangled. It can show that the first encounter was reasonable and the second wasn't. It can reveal a failure to reassess where everyone assumed a failure to diagnose. It can establish that a result was available and simply never got routed to the person responsible for it. It can separate institutional delay from an individual's clinical judgment. Most importantly, it can define the actual stretch of time during which treatment probably would have mattered. That same neutral reconstruction can just as easily show that the warning signs showed up too late, the condition progressed too quickly, or the patient was never eligible for whatever intervention supposedly would have changed things. That's exactly why timeline work has to stay neutral — the same analysis that supports a delay theory in one case can just as easily show, in another, that the alleged delay never had any real causal significance at all.

A detailed timeline can look more certain than the evidence underneath it actually is. Times get estimated. Documentation gets entered late. Different systems run on different clocks. Patients, family members, and professionals remember the sequence differently from each other. A clean diagram can draw one tidy line through a course of events that was actually uncertain and overlapping the whole time. So the timeline has to keep confirmed times separate from approximate ones, reported ones, inferred ones, disputed ones, and simply unknown ones. Precision shouldn't get manufactured just because a visual timeline looks more authoritative when every single event has an exact minute stamped next to it. The goal is understanding the sequence as accurately as the evidence allows — not making the record look more exact than it ever actually was. An honest range beats a false point of certainty every time.

Here's an example of a case where a later phone call turns out to matter more than the first symptom. A fifty-six-year-old man develops chest pressure and nausea at work. The symptoms ease after a few minutes, though he stays fatigued. He goes to an urgent-care center that afternoon. His EKG is read as showing no acute ischemic change, and his initial cardiac marker isn't elevated. He's told to go to the emergency department if the pain comes back.

A few hours later, the pain returns, more severe this time, and he calls the urgent-care center. He's told the symptoms might be gastrointestinal, and he goes to bed. The next morning he's found unresponsive, and he's diagnosed with a large myocardial infarction.

The instinct is to measure the delay from that first bout of chest pain to the eventual diagnosis. That may not be the interval that actually matters. The first visit may have been reasonably reassuring — the initial testing may have genuinely lowered the level of concern without eliminating all risk. The more important moment may be that later call, when the pain came back worse. The timeline has to establish exactly what got reported on that call, who took the message, and whether the earlier assessment was even available to that person. It has to establish what advice actually got given, and whether the patient was told to seek emergency care or not.

The causal question that follows asks whether he would have been eligible for meaningful treatment had he come in right after that call, and how much cardiac damage had already happened by then. One honest reading shows that the return of severe chest pain, on top of the earlier assessment, called for immediate emergency direction, and that the delay that followed increased the extent of the damage to his heart. Another honest reading shows entirely appropriate advice that the patient simply chose not to follow, or a major infarction that occurred later regardless and wouldn't have been prevented by any different response at that point.

The first symptom marks the start of his experience. That later call may mark the start of the delay that actually matters, clinically and legally. The treatment opportunity sits somewhere between recognition and the point where the injury became irreversible. That's the timeline this case actually needs.

Time isn't important simply because it passes. It matters because something becomes knowable, something becomes necessary, and something remains possible — and those three things don't always happen at the same moment. The first symptom may start the patient's journey. The first real warning may start a professional obligation. The point where treatment can no longer change the outcome may end the causal opportunity entirely. A useful timeline does more than count the hours. It explains what those hours actually meant.

Chapter Twelve: Obligation, Judgment, and Professional Roles

One of the easiest mistakes to make in a medical case is spotting something that could have been done differently and treating that alternative as proof the care was wrong. Medicine almost never works that neatly. There's usually more than one reasonable way to assess a patient, more than one acceptable treatment, more than one point where professional judgment simply has to be exercised. The fact that another clinician would have gone a different direction doesn't mean the path actually taken fell outside a reasonable professional range.

At the same time, "professional judgment" can't become a phrase that just ends the conversation. It can't protect a decision that ignored material information, failed to respond to a patient who was clearly changing, or kept going long after the original plan had stopped making any clinical sense. The real question was never whether another choice was possible. It's whether another response was actually required. Answering that takes looking at the patient's condition, the information available at the time, the role of the professional involved, and the authority that person genuinely held. This is one of the places law and medicine can really struggle to understand each other — the attorney needs to know what responsibility existed, and the clinician needs to explain why that responsibility arose in the first place. Both need to be clear, too, about whose responsibility it actually was.

When the outcome is severe, the earlier care can look inadequate purely because it failed to prevent what came later. That's hindsight talking. A professional's responsibility has to be judged from the point where the decision was actually made — what symptoms were present, what findings were available, which conditions were reasonably being considered, what testing had already happened, how the patient had responded to treatment so far, what resources and alternatives actually existed, and what risks came attached to those alternatives. The later diagnosis can help explain why the earlier findings mattered. It shouldn't get to replace the uncertainty that genuinely existed at the time. A patient might later be diagnosed with sepsis, a stroke, internal bleeding, something else serious — none of which means that diagnosis should have been obvious at the first visit. The better question is usually whether the presentation called for a different level of assessment, monitoring, consultation, treatment, or follow-up before the final diagnosis was ever certain. Professional responsibility can arise before diagnostic certainty does. It shouldn't get imposed simply because the eventual outcome turned out to be serious.

Medicine doesn't always produce just one correct decision. Two careful professionals can look at the same patient, choose completely different approaches, and both stay well within a reasonable range. One admits for observation; another discharges with clear precautions and prompt follow-up. One orders imaging right away; another starts with an exam, labs, or observation. One reaches for an accepted medication; another chooses a different treatment serving the same purpose. None of those alternatives existing proves that either professional acted unreasonably. A fair analysis has to identify the range of professionally supportable options before ever concluding that the chosen course fell outside it — which takes more than simply comparing the care to whatever the reviewer personally would have done. The relevant question is whether the decision stayed supportable given the circumstances actually known at the time. A review that starts and ends with someone's personal preference never actually establishes a professional obligation.

Experienced clinicians often recognize care they wouldn't have chosen themselves, and that reaction can be genuinely useful — it points toward something worth a closer look. It isn't the final standard. There's a real difference between what one clinician personally prefers, what many reasonable professionals might have done, and what the patient's actual condition required. There's also a difference between an alternative that was simply available and an alternative that became necessary because the existing plan was exposing the patient to an unacceptable risk.

Keeping those distinctions straight stops professional preference from getting dressed up as obligation, and it also stops reasonable variation in practice from becoming a blanket defense for anything. Sometimes the evidence, the seriousness of the risk, or how the patient's condition was changing leaves very little room for genuine disagreement — and when that's true, the analysis has to explain why. It's not enough to say another approach would have been better. The clinician has to show why the response actually chosen stopped being professionally supportable.

Healthcare runs through defined professional roles. A nurse, a physician, a pharmacist, a radiologist, a therapist, a technician, a consultant, an administrator — each one carries different responsibilities, and those responsibilities overlap without being interchangeable. A nurse is responsible for observing, reassessing, documenting, carrying out the care plan, and escalating a significant change — not for making the final diagnosis or independently ordering a specific treatment. A physician holds decision-making authority while depending on others to communicate changes accurately and quickly. A pharmacist can flag a medication concern without controlling the wider treatment plan. A radiologist interprets the imaging with limited information about what's happening at the bedside. A consultant offers specialty advice without taking on responsibility for coordinating or carrying out the whole plan. Before anyone criticizes the care, the analysis has to identify what that professional was actually responsible for doing — skip that step, and a case can end up blaming whoever's easiest to see instead of whoever, or whatever, actually controlled the next action.

The person who documents an event can look central purely because their name is the easiest one to find. That doesn't mean they controlled what happened next. A nurse might document worsening symptoms and notify the medical team exactly the way they're supposed to. A physician might order urgent imaging, and transport or availability might delay the scan anyway. A consultant might recommend a treatment the primary team never actually implements. A lab professional might verify a result without ever being responsible for communicating it directly to the patient. Following the actual path of responsibility, rather than how often a given name shows up, means asking who observed the problem, who received the information, who had the authority to act, who was expected to carry the decision all the way through, and where exactly the process stopped. That sequence usually matters far more than identifying whoever wrote the longest or most visible note in the chart.

Professional responsibility isn't fixed in place — it shifts as the patient moves between locations, levels of care, teams, and stages of treatment. A primary-care clinician holds responsibility while the patient is being managed in the community. The emergency department takes it over the moment the patient shows up there. An inpatient team takes over after admission. A consultant may hold responsibility for one defined specialty issue while the primary team keeps overall coordination. A covering clinician holds responsibility after hours. At discharge, some of that responsibility shifts back onto the patient, the family, an outpatient service, or a receiving facility. Those handoffs are exactly where things go wrong. Information gets left incomplete. People assume someone else is following up on a pending result. A task gets passed along without anyone clearly owning it. The patient might believe one professional is still in charge when the system has actually assigned that role somewhere else entirely. A fair review has to identify when responsibility actually changed hands, and whether that transition was actually completed safely — a handoff isn't finished just because one part of the care ended. The information, the urgency, whatever's still pending, and ownership of the follow-up all have to travel with the patient.

A lot of medical cases involve escalation — a nurse calling a physician, a clinician requesting a specialty review, a patient getting transferred to a higher level of care. An abnormal result might get routed urgently. A family member might report the patient is getting worse. Escalation was never just the act of passing information along. It requires giving the next person enough to actually understand how serious the concern is. Saying a patient "doesn't look right" can communicate real urgency in one setting and sound far too vague in another. A consult request can get entered as routine even though the patient genuinely needs to be seen right away. A consultant might get called without ever being told the patient is deteriorating, or a physician might receive one abnormal finding without the broader trend that actually makes it significant. So the analysis has to look at whether escalation happened at all, and whether it actually preserved the clinical meaning of the concern being raised. An escalation that loses the urgency, the context, or the pattern along the way may not really have functioned as an escalation at all.

Responsibility doesn't end with whoever sent the message. The professional or system receiving the information has to acknowledge it, interpret it, prioritize it, and act on it. A critical lab result can get transmitted perfectly and still sit untouched in a queue. A nurse can notify a physician, and the response can still fail to address whatever concern was actually raised. A specialist can receive a referral and miss its urgency simply because the information they were given was incomplete. A patient can report worsening symptoms and get routine advice with no real reassessment behind it. The review can't stop the moment it's established that a message got sent. It has to ask what happened once that message actually arrived — was it received by the right person? Was its significance understood? Was an appropriate decision made? Was that decision carried out, and was the patient reassessed afterward? Communication is a pathway. It's never just a single event.

Policies and procedures can offer real evidence of how an organization intended care to run — who's supposed to review an abnormal result, when escalation is required, what monitoring should happen, how a transfer or a particular clinical risk is supposed to be managed. That can clarify professional roles and how the institutional safeguards were designed. A policy isn't automatically the professional standard in every situation, though — it can be outdated, more demanding than ordinary practice actually requires, poorly implemented, or simply inapplicable to the event under review. A deviation from it can still matter a great deal, especially when the policy describes a safeguard built specifically to prevent the exact harm that occurred. The question was never simply whether a policy got followed. The analysis has to figure out what the policy was actually meant to protect against, whether the deviation actually affected the care, and whether the underlying professional obligation existed independently of that policy anyway. A policy can illuminate the care pathway. It doesn't decide liability on its own.

Clinical guidelines can be useful too, summarizing the evidence and describing accepted approaches to diagnosis, treatment, monitoring, escalation. They aren't always mandatory instructions. Guidelines can allow discretion, carry exceptions, or simply not fit a particular patient because of other conditions, contraindications, an unusual presentation, or limited resources. An attorney shouldn't assume every departure from a guideline proves negligence. A clinician shouldn't wave off a relevant guideline just because professional judgment came into play. The more useful questions are whether the guideline even applied here, whether there was a reasonable basis for departing from it, and whether that basis is actually backed up by the record or the surrounding evidence. The alternative approach deserves its own scrutiny too — did it protect the patient adequately? A guideline informs the analysis. It doesn't perform the analysis for you.

Poor documentation can make perfectly reasonable care difficult to defend. It can also make genuinely concerning care hard to actually understand. An assessment can have happened without being fully written down. A professional can remember a conversation the chart never captured. A templated note can suggest a complete exam happened even when the surrounding evidence doesn't really support that. The absence of documentation doesn't always prove the care itself was absent — it does affect how confidently that care can actually be established. The reviewer has to keep two questions separate: was the care clinically appropriate, and can the available evidence actually prove it happened? Those two questions can land in different places. A documentation failure might never have directly hurt the patient, and it can still create evidentiary uncertainty, communication risk, and real concern about continuity of care. It can also stop later professionals from understanding what's already been checked, or what's still unresolved. Documentation is part of the care process. It shouldn't get confused with the care itself.

A lot of medical cases fixate on the first decision when the more important issue is what happened afterward. A patient can reasonably get treated for a common condition, and the obligation shows up once they fail to improve. A patient can reasonably get discharged, and the obligation shows up once they call back with worsening symptoms, or return unexpectedly. A procedure can be performed entirely appropriately, and the responsibility shows up once the postoperative course drifts outside the expected range. Professional judgment has to stay responsive — a decision made once doesn't stay reasonable forever just because it was supportable at the time it was made. The patient changes. New evidence shows up. Treatment can fail. Sometimes the plan has to change right along with the patient, which is exactly why reassessment so often ends up being the real decision point in a case. The first judgment may have been perfectly reasonable. Continuing to lean on it may not have been.

Sometimes the clinical judgment itself is entirely appropriate and the process of actually delivering care is what fails. A physician correctly decides the patient needs urgent antibiotics, and the medication doesn't get administered promptly. A clinician identifies the need for a transfer, and the institution fails to escalate once no receiving bed can be found. A specialist recommends close monitoring, and staffing or workflow keeps that monitoring from actually happening. This distinction matters because the case may have nothing to do with the quality of the professional's decision at all — it may be entirely about whether the system ever turned that decision into actual care. The attorney needs to understand both halves of that. The clinician should be able to explain exactly where the clinical decision-making stopped and where operational implementation began. A correct order that never reaches the patient is not completed care, which means professional responsibility and institutional responsibility can genuinely sit at different points along the very same pathway.

Medicine can't prevent every injury. A patient can deteriorate despite prompt recognition and entirely appropriate treatment. A complication can occur despite careful technique. A disease can progress despite care that meets every accepted standard. A high-risk patient with limited physiological reserve can have a poor outcome even when everyone involved responds exactly the way they should. A fair method has to be capable of concluding that the care stayed within an acceptable range, no matter how serious the result turned out to be. That conclusion isn't indifference to the patient — it's respect for the actual limits of medicine, and for what the evidence genuinely shows. A severe outcome should prompt a careful look. It shouldn't become automatic proof that the earlier care was inadequate.

The opposite point matters just as much. A known complication shouldn't end the inquiry simply because the patient was warned it might happen. When a risk is known, professionals often still carry obligations to monitor for it, recognize it, communicate it, and respond once it shows up. A patient can consent to a procedure that carries a bleeding risk — that doesn't mean worsening signs of bleeding can just get ignored. A medication can carry a recognized risk of toxicity — that risk existing doesn't remove the need for real lab monitoring or a response to actual symptoms. A postoperative complication can happen without any negligent technique at all, and a delayed recognition or rescue afterward can still be entirely unreasonable. The known risk explains why the outcome was possible in the first place. It doesn't answer whether that risk was actually managed once it materialized.

Patients sometimes refuse treatment, delay seeking care, leave before an evaluation finishes, or don't follow what they were told to do — and those facts can genuinely affect a case and its outcome. They deserve careful handling. Was the patient given enough information to actually make that decision? Were the risks explained in language they could actually understand? Did they have the capacity to understand it, and were there practical barriers in the way — cost, transportation, fear, caregiving responsibilities, access to care? Were reasonable alternatives even offered? Did the patient go looking for help again once things changed? A patient's informed refusal can limit what the professional was able to do. It doesn't necessarily end the responsibility to communicate clearly, document that conversation, and offer the safest plan still on the table. The same goes when instructions don't get followed — the analysis has to tell an informed patient choice apart from a communication failure, inadequate access, or a discharge plan that was never realistic to begin with.

Care never happens under ideal conditions. A small hospital might not have a specialist on site. Advanced imaging might not be immediately available, and a transfer bed might be hard to find anywhere nearby. Staffing might be stretched thin, and the preferred treatment might need resources that simply don't exist locally. Those realities genuinely matter when judging what could reasonably have been done — they don't automatically excuse inadequate care, either. A facility that can't provide a needed service may still be obligated to stabilize the patient, get help, escalate the concern, arrange a transfer, and support the patient properly while they wait. The question was never whether perfect resources existed somewhere. It's whether the professionals and the institution responded reasonably given the resources they actually had and the risk the patient was actually facing. Resource limitations explain the context. They don't erase the responsibility.

Not every clinician is qualified to answer every question about professional responsibility. A nurse is well positioned to evaluate nursing observation, monitoring, documentation, communication, and escalation. A surgeon is the one who needs to weigh in on operative technique. A radiologist needs to evaluate image interpretation. A pharmacist is the right call for medication verification, dosing, interactions, safety questions. A specialist may be necessary for treatment eligibility, prognosis, or the expected benefit of some intervention. This whole approach helps identify the actual question and route it to the right professional. It doesn't turn broad healthcare experience into authority across every specialty that exists. The credibility of the analysis depends, in part, on knowing exactly where one professional's expertise ends and another's needs to begin.

Telling an attorney that care "met the standard" or "fell below the standard" isn't enough for them to actually understand the case. Counsel needs to know what information mattered, which options stayed reasonable, and what response was actually required. They need to understand who held responsibility, when the obligation arose, what evidence backs up the opinion, and what the competing interpretation looks like. That reasoning is what lets counsel test the conclusion, retain the right expert, anticipate a challenge, and make a better legal call overall. Professional authority should support transparent reasoning. It shouldn't get to substitute for it. An opinion becomes far more useful once the attorney can actually follow how the professional got from the patient's condition and the information available all the way to the conclusion being offered.

A role-based analysis keeps a case from turning into a broad, undifferentiated criticism of everyone who touched it. It can identify the actual decision point and separate individual judgment from how the system carried it out. It can show that the initial care was reasonable while a later reassessment wasn't. It can reveal that one professional acted entirely appropriately within their role while some other part of the process failed around them. It can also show that the patient's outcome happened even though the care, the whole way through, stayed within a reasonable range. The result is a more focused, fairer understanding of responsibility — instead of asking who happened to be in the room when the patient deteriorated, the analysis asks who knew what, who could actually act, and where the care pathway broke down, or held up.

That kind of analysis shouldn't get too rigid, either. Professional roles overlap in practice, and healthcare teams work collaboratively far more often than any org chart suggests. A professional can have a responsibility to act even when someone else holds final authority. An institution can lean on shared responsibility in a way that leaves nobody clearly accountable for anything. Policies and job descriptions don't always reflect how the care actually operated day to day. There's also a real danger in using the phrase "professional judgment" as a way to dodge real scrutiny — a reasonable range deserves respect, and it shouldn't become an unlimited one. The question always comes back to whether the judgment was grounded in the information actually available, responsive to the material risk, and revised once the patient's condition changed. Role analysis is supposed to clarify responsibility. It shouldn't let every participant assume someone else must have been the one responsible.

Here's an example with several possible points of failure sitting inside it. An eighty-one-year-old is admitted after surgery. Overnight, they grow increasingly confused, their blood pressure starts falling, and urine output drops. The nurse documents all of this and calls the covering physician, who orders additional fluids and asks to be called if the patient gets worse. Over the next two hours, the blood pressure improves slightly, but the confusion gets more pronounced and urine output stays low. The nurse calls again. The patient is eventually transferred to intensive care with a diagnosis of septic shock.

The family believes the nurse failed to act, since the patient stayed on the ward while deteriorating. The nursing record actually shows repeated observations and two separate calls to the physician. This can't get resolved just by figuring out who was physically at the bedside. The nurse's responsibilities were to observe, reassess, document, communicate, escalate, carry out the plan, and monitor how the patient responded. The covering physician had the authority to interpret the developing pattern, examine the patient, change the treatment, and arrange a higher level of care. The institution carried its own responsibility for escalation pathways, staffing, access to urgent review, and the systems that were supposed to turn all of this into an actual response.

One honest reading shows the second nursing call failed to actually convey how serious the deterioration had become. Another shows the physician's response failing to address a pattern that was clearly developing and needed immediate attention. A systemic issue might also have delayed access to urgent review or transfer. A different honest reading shows an initial fluid response that was entirely reasonable, reassessment that happened appropriately, and a patient whose deterioration only became severe later on, through no one's fault. The outcome alone doesn't tell you who failed. The answer lives in the roles, the information each person actually had, the authority they held to act, the decisions they made, and whether the care stayed responsive as the patient's journey kept changing underneath everyone.

Professional responsibility was never automatically owned by whoever's name is easiest to find in the chart. It follows the information, the professional role, the authority actually held, and the ability to act on all of it. Another clinician might have chosen differently without the original decision being unreasonable at all. A first decision might have been entirely reasonable while a later failure to reassess wasn't. A professional might have made exactly the right clinical call while the system around them failed to carry it out. A known complication might have occurred despite genuinely good care — or it might have needed a response that simply never came. The work is figuring out which of those actually happened here. None of this replaces professional judgment. It just helps everyone see where that judgment actually belonged, what it was based on, and whether it stayed responsive to the patient the whole way through.

Chapter Thirteen: Systems, Regulation, and Institutional Responsibility

Medical care is delivered by people, and it's made possible, or made a great deal harder, by systems. A clinician can recognize a problem and enter exactly the right order. A nurse can escalate a concern exactly the way they're supposed to. A lab can produce an important result right on time. And the patient can still get hurt, because the order never got carried out, or the message never reached the right person, or the result sat in a shared queue nobody was watching, or the transfer process stalled, or nobody ever understood whose job it was to take the next step.

This is exactly where medical cases get unfairly flattened. The most visible professional gets blamed simply because their name shows up in the chart. The organization gets criticized because some policy wasn't followed. The patient's outcome gets pinned on one person, or one procedural lapse, without anyone ever looking at how the whole process actually worked. Sometimes the individual decision really was the problem. Sometimes the system was the problem. A lot of the time, both were involved at once. Clinical Intelligence's regulatory and institutional overlay was never about hunting down every policy, rule, or regulation that could conceivably apply. It's about understanding how the organization was actually supposed to protect the patient, whether that safeguard functioned, and whether its failure changed the care the patient actually received. That's a far more useful question than simply asking whether the institution technically complied with something.

A clinical decision almost never turns into patient care in a single step. A physician decides a patient needs urgent antibiotics — that decision has to become an order, the order has to reach the pharmacy, get reviewed, prepared, delivered, administered, and documented, and then the patient has to actually get reassessed to see whether it's working. An urgent lab result has to be verified, transmitted, routed, received, understood, assigned to someone, and acted on. A patient who needs a transfer first has to be recognized as needing a higher level of care, then someone has to contact the right facility, convey the urgency, get acceptance, arrange transport, and support the patient the whole time they're waiting — and if that process stalls, someone has to actually know how and when to escalate it. Every one of those stages depends on the one before it, and a failure anywhere along that chain can quietly interrupt the care. The chart can show a decision got made, and later show the patient deteriorated, while revealing almost nothing about exactly where the process broke down in between. Clinical Intelligence follows that entire pathway, asking not just what got decided, but whether the decision actually reached the patient.

Clinicians never work independently of the organizations around them. The institution decides how results get routed, how urgent findings get flagged, how staffing gets arranged, how escalation is supposed to happen. It decides how handoffs get completed, how medications get verified, how deterioration gets monitored, how a delayed transfer gets managed. It also decides who ends up responsible when the ordinary process breaks down. None of those organizational decisions ever show up directly in a patient's progress notes — they shape the care anyway. A professional might be expected to check a shared inbox holding hundreds of results. A nurse might be responsible for several unstable patients without enough support. A physician might assume another department is following up on a pending study simply because that's how the workflow usually gets described to them. A transfer process might work fine when a bed is available and have no meaningful escalation route at all for the moment every receiving facility says no. None of this is some abstract administrative concern. It becomes a clinical concern the second it affects what actually reaches the patient. The institution creates the environment where professional judgment either turns into care, or doesn't.

Policies can be genuinely valuable because they show how an organization intended a process to work. A policy might require urgent results to get acknowledged, certain clinical changes to get escalated, high-risk medication to get extra verification. It might spell out how quickly a deteriorating patient should be reviewed, or who's supposed to take responsibility for tests still pending at discharge. That helps define expected roles and identify the safeguard the institution believed it needed. It doesn't automatically answer the case. A policy can be broader than ordinary professional practice actually requires. It can be outdated, inapplicable to this particular event, or written to leave room for a lot of judgment. It can also describe a process the institution never actually gave enough staff, technology, or training to carry out reliably. The real value of any policy is in what it tells you about the risk the organization recognized, and the protection it meant to provide. The next question is always whether that protection actually worked for this patient.

Failing to follow a policy can be genuinely concerning — it can show an expected safeguard got bypassed, or that the institution's own process simply wasn't followed, and it can point to a wider problem with training, oversight, or accountability. That deviation doesn't establish every part of a legal claim on its own, though. The analysis still has to ask whether the policy even applied, what risk it was designed to prevent, who was responsible for following it, and why it wasn't. Another reasonable process might have achieved the exact same protective purpose. The missed step might have been purely administrative and had nothing to do with the patient's outcome. In another case, the deviation is the whole ballgame — a failure to acknowledge a critical result, or to assign responsibility for a deteriorating patient, can directly interrupt care. How significant it is depends on the patient's actual journey, not on the wording of the policy by itself. A missed documentation requirement and a failed clinical safeguard shouldn't get treated as though they're the same thing just because both happen to be policy deviations.

Regulatory and compliance records can show whether a process met some external requirement, and that's genuinely important — it isn't always the same thing as understanding what happened clinically. An institution can satisfy a bare minimum regulatory requirement while the patient still falls straight through a gap in the actual workflow. A process can be technically compliant and still poorly designed. The opposite happens too — a technical deficiency can exist without ever changing the patient's care or outcome at all. Which is why compliance findings have to get translated back into clinical meaning: what risk was the requirement actually meant to address? Was this patient exposed to that risk? Did the failure interfere with recognition, communication, treatment, transfer, or follow-up? Without that translation, "compliance" turns into either an empty accusation or an empty defense. A violation existing doesn't automatically prove patient harm. The absence of a violation doesn't necessarily prove the process functioned safely either.

The person named in the chart is always easier to identify than the system standing behind them. A physician signs the discharge note, so a failure to follow up on a pending result gets pinned on that physician automatically — when the actual workflow might have assigned pending-result management to some centralized team entirely. A nurse looks like they never administered a medication, when the medication actually never reached the unit at all. A clinician looks unresponsive to a message, when the electronic system actually routed that message to the wrong inbox. The individual might still carry some responsibility. The system might also have made the failure more likely, harder to see, or harder to fix. A fair analysis shouldn't pick a side too early between individual and institutional responsibility. It should just follow the process — where did the information get generated, where did it get sent, who was supposed to receive it, who actually accepted ownership, and what happened after that. Only once that pathway is actually understood can responsibility get assigned fairly.

Organizations can get blamed too broadly, too. The word "system" can turn into a way of avoiding a particular professional's own conduct. The policy might have been perfectly clear, the staffing might have been entirely adequate, and the result might have reached exactly the right person — with the actual failure sitting in the decision not to respond. Not every problem should get pushed up to the institution just because healthcare is complicated. The analysis has to identify exactly where the pathway actually broke: was the process poorly designed? Was it sound and simply not followed? Was responsibility unclear, or did someone get the information they needed and just make an unreasonable call? Were there several failures scattered across different points? The answer can be uncomfortable for either side, which is exactly why following the actual pathway matters more than starting from whichever explanation you'd prefer to land on.

Patients are usually at their most vulnerable exactly when responsibility moves from one professional or setting to another — during a shift change, a transfer between departments, a hospital discharge, a consultant getting involved, or the move from hospital care back into the community. It can happen when a result comes back after the original encounter has already ended. The person sending information can believe responsibility has already transferred. The person receiving it can believe the original team is still in charge. The patient can assume someone's tracking the issue when nobody has actually accepted ownership of it. A safe handoff takes more than just sending information along — it needs enough context for whoever's receiving it to understand what actually matters, a clear sense of who now owns the next action, and some way of confirming that responsibility has genuinely landed somewhere. A discharge summary can go out without ever flagging a pending test. A consultant can make a recommendation without ever clarifying who's supposed to actually carry it out. A primary-care office can receive a hospital record after the window for urgent follow-up has already closed. A handoff isn't complete the moment information leaves one place. It's complete once the necessary responsibility has actually arrived somewhere else.

Pending test results are a recurring source of failure precisely because the clinical encounter can end before the information's own journey does. A patient gets discharged while a culture, a pathology result, an imaging read, or a lab study is still pending. Someone has to stay responsible for watching that result, understanding what it means, contacting the patient, arranging follow-up, and documenting all of it — and the chart doesn't always make clear who that someone actually is. The ordering clinician might assume the primary-care office will follow up on the result. The primary-care office might not even know the test was ordered. A centralized team might only handle certain categories of results. The patient might get an automated notification with no way to understand how urgent it actually is or what they're supposed to do next. A pending-result case has to get analyzed as a whole process, not just as one missed phone call — the real question is whether the system actually closed the loop from the result being generated all the way to some completed action.

Electronic systems lean heavily on shared queues, pools, inboxes, task lists — tools that can genuinely improve efficiency by letting several people access the same work. They can just as easily create ambiguity. When a result is visible to a lot of people, each one can assume someone else will handle it. When responsibility belongs to a team instead of a named individual, ownership can get genuinely fuzzy. The system might show that a result entered the queue. It might not show that anyone actually accepted responsibility for it. Availability is not the same thing as accountability — a result everyone can technically see can still belong to no one at all. The institution needs an actual process that identifies ownership, prioritizes urgent items, and confirms things got done. Without that structure, a shared queue can create the illusion of access without any of the reality of responsibility.

Electronic alerts get talked about as though they've solved the whole communication problem. They haven't, not always. An alert can fail to fire, land with the wrong person, or get buried among a mountain of routine warnings. It can get acknowledged without the underlying issue ever actually getting addressed. It can also stay active after someone's already dealt with it, creating confusion about whether the task still belongs to somebody else. Alert fatigue isn't a justification for ignoring critical information — it's also not solved by simply bolting more alerts onto an already overloaded system. The review has to ask whether a given alert was actually meaningful, actionable, assigned to someone, and built into the real workflow. Did it convey real urgency? Did whoever received it understand what was actually required? Did acknowledging it mean responsibility had genuinely been accepted, or just that a button got clicked? Technology should support safe communication. It shouldn't create the illusion of safety instead.

Staffing comes up constantly when institutional responsibility is on the table, and it has to get connected back to the actual patient to mean anything. A low staffing number doesn't automatically prove the care was unreasonable. A poor outcome doesn't automatically prove staffing caused it. The review has to identify the actual clinical effect — was monitoring done less often than the patient's condition required? Was escalation delayed because nobody was available to reassess? Was medication given late? Was a significant change missed because one staff member was responsible for an unsafe number, or mix, of patients? Did the patient need a level of observation the unit simply couldn't provide? The staffing question only becomes useful once it's tied to a specific part of the care pathway. Otherwise it just stays a general complaint about the organization instead of an actual explanation of what happened to the patient.

An institution can have a policy and still fail to train people on how to use it. Training can exist without ever producing real competence. Competence can exist while the system keeps a professional from actually applying it reliably. These are three genuinely different problems. A staff member might not understand how to escalate an urgent result. A team might misunderstand who actually owns a shared queue. A new electronic system might get rolled out without enough preparation. A specialty pathway might sit in a manual somewhere while remaining a complete mystery to frontline staff. The question was never simply whether training happened. It's whether the people responsible could actually use the process effectively at the moment the patient needed them to. A completed training record doesn't prove a safeguard functioned. The real test is whether the expected action could actually get carried out safely in practice.

Healthcare professionals build workarounds constantly, whenever the official process is slow, unclear, or unreliable — handwritten notes, informal messages, personal reminders, unofficial tracking systems of their own invention. Those workarounds can genuinely keep patients safe. They can also create hidden risk. When an institution ends up depending on one person simply remembering to compensate for a flawed process, the whole system can fail the moment that person is out sick, overwhelmed, or unfamiliar with the workaround in the first place. The written policy shows how the system was supposed to work. The workaround often shows how it actually worked, and both of those things can matter. A workaround isn't automatically evidence of wrongdoing — it can just as easily reflect professionals adapting practically to protect their patients. It can also reveal that the official safeguard was never reliable enough to actually do its job.

Institutions don't have unlimited resources. A hospital might lack an on-site specialist, an ICU bed, an advanced imaging service, or some particular treatment capability — and that limitation can be entirely real. The obligation then becomes about recognition, stabilization, escalation, transfer, communication. The absence of a resource doesn't create some magical ability to provide something the institution simply doesn't have. It can create a responsibility to respond reasonably precisely because that resource isn't available. Was the limitation known ahead of time? Was the patient accepted despite it? Was a transfer started promptly? Were reasonable alternatives actually considered? Was the patient monitored and supported adequately while everyone waited? The resource limitation is part of the clinical setting. The institution's response to that limitation is part of the case. A lack of resources can explain why one course of action was impossible. It doesn't automatically explain why no effective alternative was ever pursued.

An organization can hold important information across several departments even when no single professional ever pulled it together. The lab system holds the abnormal result. The nursing record shows the deterioration. The pharmacy system shows repeated medication changes. Staffing records show limited capacity to respond, while transfer logs reveal a long, drawn-out struggle to find a bed. Taken together, the institution might genuinely possess a clear picture of what was happening. Individually, nobody actually saw all of it at once. Which raises a genuinely hard question: when should a system be designed to connect information that no individual clinician could reasonably hold in their head alone? There's no universal answer to that. The more foreseeable and serious the risk, though, the more that reliable integration starts to matter. A healthcare system can't just assume fragmented information will somehow become meaningful on its own — it has to decide which patterns actually need connecting, who's responsible for seeing them, and how escalation happens once the risk climbs. At the same time, the analysis has to avoid unfairly loading institutional knowledge onto one clinician who genuinely never had access to the whole picture. Individual and institutional knowledge are related. They aren't interchangeable.

A lot of regulatory requirements and accreditation standards exist because specific failures are already known to put patients at risk — medication safety, infection control, result communication, patient identification, handoffs, staffing, emergency preparedness, quality review, adverse-event reporting. That history helps explain why a given safeguard matters. It still has to get applied carefully. A broad regulatory standard may not spell out the precise professional obligation in this one patient's case — its relevance often lies in showing the recognized risk, the expected institutional response, and whether the organization's process was actually capable of providing that protection. Regulation gives context to the safeguard. Patient-specific evidence shows whether the failure actually mattered here. The two need to stay connected without getting confused for each other.

Institutions sometimes write up internal reports after something goes wrong. Those reports can hold genuinely useful information about timing, communication, process failures, corrective action — flagging concerns that never show up in the ordinary chart. They're also limited by their own purpose, timing, legal status, and whatever information the person writing them actually had. An incident report shouldn't get treated automatically as a full admission, or as some perfectly objective reconstruction of events. It can identify a possible process problem without settling the clinical or causal questions at all, and counsel still has to weigh the legal rules around access, privilege, discoverability, use. Clinically, the report can still be useful, because it shows exactly where the organization itself believed further examination was warranted. It's one source of evidence. It's not the final word on what happened.

After something goes wrong, an institution might revise a policy, add an alert, retrain staff, change a workflow. That can show the organization spotted an opportunity to reduce future risk. It doesn't automatically prove the earlier process was unreasonable. Organizations change for all kinds of reasons — new evidence, new technology, greater awareness, or simply wanting a stronger safeguard than before. How much weight that corrective action carries, and how it can actually be used in a case, depends on the circumstances and the governing law. Clinical Intelligence can explain what actually changed operationally and why that change might matter clinically. Counsel still has to work out how that information can actually be used in the case. A later improvement shouldn't get automatically converted into an admission about the past.

A poorly designed system, on its own, doesn't establish that it caused this patient's injury. The analysis has to circle back to the patient's actual journey: what information failed to move? What action didn't happen, and how long did that failure last? What treatment or intervention remained available during that stretch? What difference probably followed from it? A systems issue only becomes causally meaningful once it actually changes the care in a way that changes the outcome. Without that connection, the whole analysis is just organizational criticism dressed up as something more. The same principle protects both sides equally — a genuinely serious institutional weakness can exist without ever having caused the harm being claimed, and a seemingly small process failure can end up being the whole case, once it interrupts time-sensitive care. How much a systems issue matters gets measured by its actual effect on the patient. Nothing else.

A systems-based review can explain why an individual professional looks like they failed when they really didn't. It can identify unclear responsibility, show how a genuinely sound clinical decision got poorly implemented, and reveal a process that kept exposing patients to the exact same risk over and over. It can show that the institution actually had the necessary information and simply lacked a reliable way to connect it. It can just as easily show that the system worked exactly as intended and the adverse outcome happened anyway, despite every safeguard doing its job. The point was never to make every case about the institution. It's to figure out whether the organization shaped the care that actually reached this patient. Systems analysis earns its keep when it clarifies the patient's journey — not when it balloons the case out into every possible organizational grievance imaginable.

This kind of review can get too broad very quickly. Once the inquiry expands into policies, staffing, regulation, technology, training, communication, and oversight all at once, it's easy to lose the patient entirely. Not every institutional weakness is relevant. Not every regulation actually applies, and not every process deviation changed the care that got delivered. The reviewer should resist the urge to build a whole catalogue of organizational imperfections. The actual work is identifying the small handful of safeguards and process points that genuinely mattered to this patient's journey: what should have protected this patient? Did it work? When it failed, did that failure actually change recognition, communication, treatment, or follow-up? Staying that focused is what keeps the analysis proportionate, and useful.

Here's an example of a result that belonged to everyone, and to no one. A sixty-nine-year-old has outpatient imaging after several weeks of worsening abdominal symptoms. The radiology report identifies a suspicious mass and recommends urgent specialist follow-up. The result gets finalized on a Friday afternoon.

The ordering office uses a shared results queue. The report lands in the queue, and nobody in particular gets assigned to it. An automated notification also goes out to the patient portal. The patient sees a result is available and doesn't understand the medical language, or how urgent it is. No one actually reaches out to them directly. Three weeks later, they show up at an emergency department with an obstruction and get diagnosed with advanced cancer.

The first impression is that the ordering clinician simply ignored the report. The wider evidence shows the clinician was actually away when the result came back. Covering staff were supposed to check the shared queue, and the process never actually assigned anyone individual ownership of it. The radiology system had classified the finding as significant but not immediately critical. The patient portal delivered the report with no plain-language explanation and no clear instruction about follow-up.

Several separate questions now need separate answers. Did the ordering office have a reliable process for covering results while someone was out? Who was actually supposed to be responsible during that absence? Was the radiology classification reasonable, and was a portal notification alone really enough for a finding that needed urgent follow-up? The causal question, kept separate from all of that, asks whether the mass was already advanced enough that the three-week gap made no real difference — the delay might have contributed to an emergency presentation without ever actually changing the eventual stage or prognosis.

One honest reading shows an organization with no reliable closed-loop process, and a delay that allowed real progression, worsened the obstruction, or narrowed the treatment options that remained. Another honest reading shows a cancer whose stage and prognosis would have ended up the same regardless, a result that never actually required emergency intervention, or a patient who'd already been told to arrange follow-up and simply didn't. The systemic problem here can be completely clear while its actual causal effect stays genuinely uncertain. Both questions still need answering.

Patients don't receive decisions. They receive care only once those decisions actually make it, successfully, through the people and systems standing between the decision and the bedside. A result has to reach someone who understands what it means. A concern has to get communicated with enough context to keep its urgency intact. An order has to actually get carried out. A transfer has to actually get completed, and the patient has to actually get reassessed. When that chain breaks somewhere, responsibility can belong to one individual, to the institution, or to the way the two interacted with each other. Clinical Intelligence helps identify exactly where the process actually stopped, without assuming the answer just from whichever name happens to be sitting in the chart, or whichever policy happens to be sitting in the manual. The institution matters because it creates the conditions where professional judgment either reaches the patient, or doesn't.

Chapter Fourteen: Causation as the Meeting Point of Law and Medicine

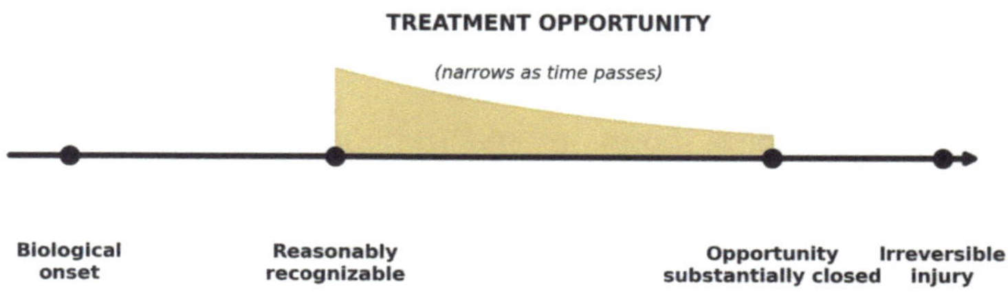

Figure 14.1 — Recognizability, treatment opportunity, and irreversible injury over time

Causation is where a lot of medical cases either come together or start falling apart. It's also where law and medicine are most likely to believe they're discussing the same issue when they genuinely aren't. A clinician says a delay contributed to the patient's decline. The attorney hears proof that the delay caused the injury. An expert believes earlier treatment offered a possibility of benefit, while counsel walks away believing the outcome probably would have been prevented. Those differences aren't minor wording issues. They shape whether a case should proceed, what damages can fairly be attributed, what expert opinion is actually needed, and how the evidence should get explained to the client. Causation isn't just a concluding sentence tacked onto the end of a medical review. It's the point where the patient's clinical journey has to get translated into a supportable explanation of what actually happened. What occurred biologically? What response should reasonably have followed? What treatment opportunity remained, and what probably would have changed? What part of the outcome was already likely regardless, because of the patient's own underlying condition? Medicine and law have to meet around those questions without ever becoming interchangeable — the clinician explains the medical pathway, the qualified expert provides the necessary opinion, and the attorney figures out how that opinion fits inside the governing law. Clinical Intelligence gives all of them the same pathway to actually examine.

A huge amount of causal reasoning starts with pure sequence. The patient got medication and later developed bleeding. A diagnosis got delayed, and the patient deteriorated. Surgery happened, followed by a complication. A result never got acted on, and the disease progressed. That sequence can be genuinely important. It doesn't prove causation by itself. One event can follow another without being the reason the second one happened — the patient may have had underlying disease that was already progressing regardless. The complication may have been a well-recognized risk of otherwise appropriate treatment. The injury may already have been set in motion before the alleged delay even began. Several different factors can be operating at once. Sequence tells you where to start investigating. Causation is the explanation of the relationship — and that distinction matters because a chronology can make a causal link look obvious purely by proximity. The closer two events sit together in time, the easier it is to treat one as the explanation for the other. The clinical evidence still has to actually show why that relationship makes medical sense, and what difference the disputed care probably made.

A causal theory that's actually supportable needs a medically plausible mechanism — some explanation of how the disputed act or omission could have produced the harm being pinned on it. In a case involving delayed treatment of an infection, the mechanism might involve continued bacterial growth, rising inflammation, reduced tissue perfusion, organ injury. In delayed stroke recognition, it might involve ongoing loss of brain tissue during a window when effective treatment remained available. A medication-related bleeding case might need to weigh the drug's effect on clotting, the dose, interactions, monitoring, timing, and the patient's own existing vulnerability. A pressure-injury case might involve immobility, tissue perfusion, moisture, nutrition, how long the pressure lasted, and whether repositioning and skin protection were adequate. The mechanism doesn't always reduce to one clean straight line — medical outcomes are often messier than that. It still has to connect the disputed care to the actual injury in a way that fits this patient, this timing, this evidence. A theory that's biologically possible in general can still fall apart when you actually try to apply it to this specific case.

A lot of things are medically possible. A medication can be capable of causing a particular injury without being the most likely cause in this particular patient. A delay can be capable of worsening an outcome even when the evidence can't show it probably did so here. A traumatic event can be capable of aggravating spinal disease while the patient's later symptoms are actually better explained by natural progression. A clinician might be able to point to a plausible relationship. An expert may still need to determine whether that relationship is probable enough to actually support the opinion being asked for. The attorney needs to understand that gap — the question was never just whether the proposed mechanism can happen. It's whether that mechanism explains this patient's outcome more convincingly than the reasonable alternatives sitting next to it. Possibility opens the inquiry. Probability is what gives the causal opinion any real, usable meaning.

Causation asks us to imagine a course of events that never actually happened — what probably would have occurred if the care had been different. That's the counterfactual, and it can't be observed directly. It has to be built out of the patient's baseline, the disease process, the treatment that was available, the timing, the outcome evidence, and a qualified clinician's judgment. The counterfactual has to stay realistic — it shouldn't assume perfect care, a perfect recovery, or a patient with no pre-existing disease at all. It should ask what probably would have happened to this actual patient under whatever reasonable alternative is actually being proposed. Would the whole injury have been avoided? Would it have been less severe? Would treatment simply have started earlier without changing the final outcome at all? Would the patient have lived longer, needed less invasive treatment, recovered more function, avoided some amount of long-term care? The causal conclusion needs to match whatever that comparison actually shows. Without a realistic counterfactual, the whole analysis risks comparing the real patient against some imaginary ideal outcome instead of the probable alternative course that actually existed.

It's not enough to say the care should have been better, or that something should have happened sooner. What, specifically, should have happened instead? Should the patient have been admitted rather than discharged? Should imaging have been repeated, antibiotics started, a specialist called? Should a result have been communicated directly to someone? Should the patient have been transferred, or should a medication have been withheld, adjusted, or monitored differently? Causation can't really get tested until that alternative action is actually spelled out clearly. And the proposed alternative has to have been reasonable given what actually existed at the time — a treatment that was unavailable, contraindicated, or simply not clinically indicated can't become the causal answer just because the eventual outcome turned out to be severe. Defining the alternative is what lets the analysis move from criticism into an actual comparison: would that particular response, at that particular time, probably have changed the patient's course?

A treatment can exist and still not be available to this particular patient. Eligibility genuinely matters. The patient may have shown up too late. Imaging may already have shown established injury, or some contraindication may have made the intervention unsafe. The expected risk may have outweighed the likely benefit. The patient may have refused treatment after being properly informed. The facility may simply not have offered the intervention at all, which raises its own separate question about recognition, stabilization, consultation, transfer. A general claim that earlier treatment improves outcomes on average isn't enough — the analysis has to determine whether this specific patient probably could have received, and benefited from, the intervention at the relevant time. That question usually needs real specialty expertise, and often needs original imaging, precise clinical timing, lab evidence, and a clear picture of the patient's baseline and other conditions. Without patient-specific eligibility established, the proposed alternative just stays theoretical.

Delay can sound powerful, because it hands the case a measurable stretch of time. The more important question is what actually remained capable of being changed during that stretch. A six-hour delay might have almost no causal effect if the injury was already irreversible. A forty-five-minute delay might be enormously significant if the patient was sitting inside a narrow, meaningful treatment window the whole time. Which is exactly why causation should focus on the treatment opportunity rather than the delay by itself. When did the need for a different response become reasonably recognizable? What intervention remained available at that point? How did the expected benefit shrink as time passed? When did the opportunity start narrowing, or close entirely? What additional harm developed in the gap between the actual response and the reasonable alternative? Those questions tie time to outcome. Without them, delay stays just a description of what happened, rather than an actual explanation of what it caused.

Medical cases often get discussed in all-or-nothing terms — either the event caused the injury or it didn't, either the outcome would have been prevented or it would have happened anyway regardless. A lot of patient journeys simply don't fit that shape. Earlier treatment might not have prevented the disease and still might have reduced how severe the injury got. A complication might have happened no matter what, while earlier recognition could have shortened how long the patient stayed critically ill. A patient might ultimately have died from advanced disease, and delayed care might still have shortened their survival or increased their suffering along the way. A pre-existing condition might account for part of a disability while the disputed event genuinely made it materially worse. The causal role deserves to be described as precisely as the evidence actually allows — sometimes that's complete prevention, sometimes it's reduced severity, aggravation, acceleration, a longer recovery, a heavier treatment burden, greater care needs, shortened survival, temporary worsening, or, sometimes, no material difference at all. A narrower conclusion isn't automatically a weaker one. It can be the most accurate, most defensible conclusion actually available.

Pre-existing disease shouldn't get parked outside the causation analysis as though it only matters for calculating damages. It can shape the entire pathway. A vulnerable patient may have been more likely to deteriorate even with entirely appropriate care — and that same vulnerability may have raised the need for monitoring and early intervention in the first place. A patient with advanced vascular disease might have had a worse stroke despite prompt treatment, and that same disease might be exactly why timely treatment mattered so much. A patient with severe spinal degeneration might have been more susceptible to injury, and the later event might still have produced a genuine, material change in symptoms, function, or treatment need. The question was never simply whether pre-existing disease existed. It's how that disease actually interacted with the disputed event and the final outcome. Baseline and causation can't really be pulled apart from each other — the patient's earlier condition is what helps explain both what was already likely to happen, and what actually changed because of the event.

A strong causal analysis takes on the best competing explanation available, not the easiest one to wave away. The patient may have experienced natural disease progression, an unavoidable complication, a delayed presentation, medication effects, another traumatic event, an unrelated infection. Limited physiological reserve may have played a real role. Several of these causes may have been operating together at once. Another cause existing doesn't automatically sink the case — it can reduce the share of the outcome that can fairly be pinned on the disputed care, or it can show the disputed care made no material difference at all. What actually matters is how much of the outcome that competing explanation accounts for, and a fair review should say so directly, rather than mentioning alternative causes in passing and then proceeding as if they don't change anything. Competing explanations have to carry real weight in how strong, and how broad, the final causal conclusion gets to be.

Medicine is genuinely comfortable with outcomes that have several causes at once. Litigation sometimes pushes hard toward naming one dominant cause instead. The patient's actual journey may hold several causes at the same time, and that's fine. An older patient might sustain a hip fracture in a fall, develop surgical complications, get an infection, and lose their independence through the combined weight of trauma, illness, frailty, and prolonged immobility all acting together. A patient with chronic vascular disease might suffer an evolving stroke, experience delayed recognition, and end up with limited recovery because of both the original disease and the treatment opportunity that got lost along the way. None of this requires erasing every factor but one. It requires identifying the additional difference the disputed care probably made — which is exactly where the medical explanation turns into something legally useful. It lets the case recognize a genuine causal contribution without pretending the disputed conduct explains the patient's entire condition from top to bottom.

The word "contributed" gets used constantly when several factors are involved, and it's often accurate without being remotely clear enough on its own. How did the care actually contribute? Did it make the injury bigger or more severe? Did it prolong low oxygen, delay control of an infection, increase blood loss, or reduce mobility in a way that led to further complications? Did it shorten the time the patient otherwise would have had? Did it increase the treatment burden or how much care the patient needed afterward? The word needs to be followed by the actual difference it made. Without that, "contributed" can sound important while remaining genuinely impossible for an attorney to evaluate or use. A useful causal opinion describes the actual clinical consequence of the contribution — not just the fact that a contribution supposedly existed.

Aggravation can't really be understood without a real baseline sitting underneath it. The patient had a condition before the event, and it looked different afterward — the analysis has to explain exactly what changed. Did the pain get more severe, or constant? Was function lost? Did treatment need to escalate, did surgery become necessary sooner than it otherwise would have, did new care needs show up? The pre-existing condition should stay visible the whole time. So should the additional harm. A fair aggravation analysis doesn't describe the entire condition as brand new, and it doesn't dismiss a genuinely new limitation just because the underlying structure was already abnormal to begin with. The causal opinion has to identify the added burden the event actually created.

Acceleration is fundamentally a question of timing — it means the patient reached some level of decline, disability, treatment, or death sooner than would otherwise have been expected. That conclusion needs some real sense of the likely prior course. A patient with progressive disease may have been expected to worsen eventually regardless — the disputed event may simply have moved that decline forward in time. The real question becomes how much earlier, and with what consequences. The answer doesn't have to be exact. It should still get examined wherever the evidence actually supports it, because acceleration can be clinically and legally meaningful even when the final condition was always likely to happen at some later point anyway. The causal difference here might just be the loss of months, or years, of independence — not the creation of a condition that would never otherwise have developed at all.

Some cases turn on a reduced chance of recovery or survival rather than a cleanly preventable outcome. This is a legally sensitive area, and how it gets treated varies by jurisdiction — the clinical analysis shouldn't assume a reduced opportunity gets recognized, or measured, the same way everywhere. The medical question underneath it can still matter enormously. Did the delay reduce the patient's likelihood of benefiting from treatment? Was that reduction small, or substantial? Was the patient already unlikely to recover regardless? Did the proposed intervention offer only a remote possibility, or a genuinely meaningful probability? The expert should explain the clinical effect plainly. The attorney has to work out how the governing law actually treats that effect. Clinical Intelligence keeps those two roles separate, while making sure the clinical question never gets lost simply because its legal treatment happens to vary from place to place.

Research showing that earlier treatment is associated with better outcomes on average can support an analysis. It doesn't prove what would have happened to one specific patient. Population studies describe groups. This individual patient may differ from that group because of age, disease severity, baseline function, anatomy, other conditions, timing, contraindications, complications. An expert can use population evidence as part of their reasoning — the conclusion still has to come back around to this patient specifically. General benefit has to get translated into patient-specific probability. A study showing better average outcomes with earlier treatment doesn't establish that the treatment would probably have changed things for someone who was ineligible, who showed up too late, or who already had irreversible injury by the time anyone could act. Research informs the pathway. It doesn't replace it.

A study showing that some factor is associated with a higher rate of injury doesn't necessarily establish that the factor caused this patient's injury. The association might be shaped by other variables entirely. The study population might not resemble this patient at all, and the measured outcome might differ from the harm actually being alleged. The size of the reported effect might be modest to begin with. Statistical evidence can strengthen or weaken a causal opinion — it shouldn't get used as a substitute for actual clinical reasoning. Attribution needs the evidence to connect that general relationship to this individual patient's mechanism, timing, baseline, and outcome.

A useful causation opinion doesn't just declare that the event caused the injury and stop there. It explains the relevant baseline, the underlying disease or injury process, and the disputed act or omission. It identifies the reasonable alternative response, the treatment opportunity, the patient's eligibility, and the probable benefit. It addresses the competing causes honestly, and it describes the specific outcome difference at stake. That reasoning is what lets the attorney actually understand what the opinion supports, and it's what lets another expert challenge the right part of the pathway instead of arguing in circles. An unexplained conclusion can sound powerful. It's hard to test and even harder to defend. Professional authority matters here, and it shouldn't be allowed to substitute for transparent reasoning.

The strength of the wording used should always reflect the strength of the foundation underneath it. Where the evidence is strong, the opinion shouldn't hide behind vague language just to sound cautious. Where the evidence is limited, the opinion shouldn't sound certain just to sound useful. Depending on the evidence and the professional context, an opinion might say the findings are consistent with a relationship, support a relationship, probably contributed to the outcome, or more likely than not increased the severity of harm. It might conclude the event likely aggravated the condition, that the causal components can't be reliably separated, or that the available evidence simply doesn't support a material causal relationship. The exact legal phrasing can shift by jurisdiction and purpose. The underlying clinical meaning has to stay clear regardless. Words shouldn't get chosen because they sound persuasive. They should communicate what the evidence actually supports, no more and no less.

Not every causal question can get resolved precisely. The onset may be uncertain. The treatment window may be an estimate rather than a known fact, and the patient's likely response may only be knowable as a range. Experts may reasonably disagree. Important evidence may simply be missing. That uncertainty doesn't always end the analysis, and it has to actually affect the conclusion — the opinion may need to get narrower, the confidence lower, or more evidence may need to be gathered before anyone relies on it. In some cases, the uncertainty may make continuing the litigation hard to justify at all. The important principle is that uncertainty has to stay visible, and it has to have real consequences — it can't get acknowledged in one paragraph and then quietly ignored by the time the conclusion shows up.

Clinical Intelligence was never meant to approach causation as though its whole job is connecting every professional departure to some harm. Sometimes the honest analysis shows the outcome was already unavoidable — the condition may have progressed too far before the patient ever sought care. The patient may never have been eligible for the treatment being proposed. The alleged delay may have happened after the meaningful treatment opportunity had already closed. The injury may be better explained by the underlying disease. A process failure may have occurred without ever actually changing the outcome. Those findings can be entirely decisive, and they deserve to be stated with exactly the same clarity as findings that support the claim. A fair method has to be able to identify a real failure and still conclude, honestly, that it caused no material harm.

The evidence may not support that the entire outcome would have been prevented, and that doesn't always mean the case has no supportable causal theory left. The attributable harm might involve additional organ damage, a longer hospital stay, more invasive treatment, a worse recovery, or greater ongoing care needs. It might involve a shorter survival, more suffering, or a longer stretch of rehabilitation. Counsel may decide the narrower version of the case still holds up. The client deserves to understand that shift, and the damages analysis should follow right along with it. A causal theory actually gets stronger the moment it stops claiming harm the evidence can't support. Precision isn't retreat. It's credibility.

The causal role described internally on a case has to match the role presented to the expert, the client, the opposing side, the mediator, and the court. A case shouldn't start out as aggravation and quietly get presented later as complete causation with no new supporting evidence behind that shift. A preliminary possibility shouldn't turn into a probability just because it's been repeated enough times. The language can evolve as new evidence comes in — the reasoning behind that evolution has to stay traceable the whole way through. Staying consistent is what lets counsel actually understand what the case is claiming, and it's what keeps the clinical meaning from quietly inflating as it moves deeper into litigation.

A structured look at causation stops a case from jumping straight from "failure" to "injury" without anything connecting the two. It identifies the alternative care actually being proposed and tests whether the patient could genuinely have received it, and benefited from it. It puts competing causes at the center of the analysis instead of the margins, and lets a limited or partial causal role get described accurately instead of rounded up or down. It helps counsel figure out which expert is actually needed and what question that expert has to answer. The analysis might strengthen a claim, support a defense, narrow a theory, or show that more work isn't likely to change the conclusion either way. Its value is in making the pathway visible.

Causation diagrams and structured pathways can make uncertainty look tidier than it actually is. A patient's biology doesn't always follow a straight line. More than one mechanism can be plausible at once, and the treatment opportunity may never have had clean, obvious boundaries. Population evidence can get applied with more confidence than it deserves. An expert can reach beyond what the actual records support, or technology can generate causal-sounding language simply because one event happened to follow another. The analysis has to stay anchored to the source evidence, the patient-specific facts, real expertise, and clearly stated uncertainty. A structured pathway is genuinely useful. It shouldn't be allowed to make a causal case look more settled than it actually is.

Here's an example that needs a lot more than sequence to make sense of it. A sixty-three-year-old with atrial fibrillation and vascular disease develops sudden weakness and trouble speaking at home. The family calls emergency services, and the patient reaches the hospital during what could have been an important treatment window. The initial exam documents partial improvement. Imaging shows no hemorrhage, and the patient gets admitted for observation instead of immediate stroke-directed treatment. Several hours later, the neurological deficits get worse, and repeat imaging shows a large ischemic stroke.

The initial allegation is that treatment should have started immediately and would have prevented the stroke. The causal analysis needs considerably more than that. Was the patient actually eligible for the treatment being proposed? How severe and disabling were the initial symptoms, really? Did that partial improvement make the original decision reasonable at the time? Were there contraindications, and what did the vascular imaging actually show? When did the larger injury actually develop, and what outcome probably would have followed with earlier treatment?

One honest reading shows the patient remained eligible, the original deficits were clinically significant, and earlier treatment probably would have reduced the size and severity of the stroke. Another honest reading shows symptoms that were genuinely mild or rapidly improving, treatment risk that was substantial, or vascular findings that limited how much benefit was ever realistically on the table. The evidence might support reduced severity rather than complete prevention. It might support no material difference at all. None of that answer comes from the simple fact that treatment wasn't given and the patient later got worse. It has to come from the complete causal pathway, examined honestly.

Causation was never the statement that one event happened and another followed. It's the explanation of what probably changed because the care that was actually given differed from what reasonably should have happened. That explanation starts with the patient's baseline. It needs a real, defined alternative response rather than a vague claim that the care could have been better. It depends on timing, treatment eligibility, and whatever opportunity actually remained. It has to account for harm that was already likely regardless, and for whatever other causes were operating alongside the disputed event. Sometimes the answer really is complete prevention. More often, it's narrower than that. Sometimes there's no supportable causal difference at all, and that has to be an acceptable answer too. Law and medicine meet at causation because neither profession can answer the whole question alone. Medicine explains the pathway. Law decides what that pathway actually allows the case to become.

Acknowledgements

This book grew from many years of working within healthcare, reviewing difficult cases, and trying to understand why the same patient journey could look so different depending on who was reading the record.

I want to acknowledge the attorneys and clinicians whose questions, disagreements, insights, and professional experience helped shape the thinking behind this work. The differences between law and medicine are real, but so is the value created when both professions are willing to listen carefully, explain their reasoning, and remain open to what the evidence may actually show.

I am especially grateful to the professionals who have recognized that collaboration does not weaken expertise. It strengthens it. Attorneys should not be expected to become clinicians, and clinicians should not be expected to become attorneys. The best work occurs when each profession contributes what it understands while respecting the judgment and responsibility of the other.

I also want to acknowledge the patients and families whose experiences sit behind every medical record. Their journeys are often divided across notes, departments, systems, and institutions, but their experience was never fragmented. It was one continuous story. This book was written with the hope that those stories can be understood more fully and evaluated more fairly.

My thanks also go to everyone who has supported the development of Lexcura Summit and the wider Clinical Intelligence methodology. Building something new requires patience, challenge, honest feedback, and the willingness to continue when the path is not yet obvious. Each conversation, question, and contribution has helped bring greater clarity to the work.

I am deeply grateful to my family for their encouragement and for the many ways they have supported me while this work continued to grow.

Writing a book, building a company, and developing a new body of thought require time and persistence, and that work is never completed entirely alone.

Finally, I want to thank the readers of this book. Whether you come to it as an attorney, clinician, expert, consultant, educator, or another professional working with medically complex cases, I hope it helps you see the evidence differently.

More importantly, I hope it helps you see the patient more clearly within it.

About the Author

Michelle Carroll is the Founder and Chief Clinical Strategist of Lexcura Summit, where she has developed the concept of Clinical Intelligence as a practical way to help legal and clinical professionals understand medically complex cases more clearly.

Her work is shaped by more than forty years of experience in healthcare and by a longstanding interest in the point where clinical understanding and legal decision-making meet. Over time, she became increasingly aware that attorneys and clinicians were often reviewing the same records, discussing the same patient, and still reaching the case from very different directions.

Clinical Intelligence grew from that observation.

It was not created to replace the judgment of attorneys, clinicians, or qualified experts. It developed through years of asking why important information was being missed, how the patient's journey became lost within the record, and what was needed to help different professionals understand the same evidence without stepping outside their own expertise.

Through Lexcura Summit, Michelle's work focuses on patient-centered analysis, medical evidence, case evaluation, professional education, and the development of structured methods that support fairer and better-informed litigation decisions.

She is the author of a growing body of work on Clinical Intelligence, including its use in personal injury, medical malpractice, mass tort, and other medically complex litigation. Her writing is intended to make difficult medical evidence more accessible without oversimplifying it and to encourage stronger collaboration between the professionals responsible for interpreting it.

At the center of that work is a simple belief: the patient lived one journey, and the evidence should be understood in a way that allows law and medicine to meet around that same experience.

Michelle is the Founder of Lexcura Summit, whose mission is expressed through the guiding principle:

Clinical Intelligence for Better Litigation Decisions™

www.ingramcontent.com/pod-product-compliance
Lightning Source LLC
LaVergne TN
LVHW051157210926
848486LV00006B/291

* 9 7 9 8 9 5 2 0 9 4 1 3 0 *